Pray & Play

Pray & Play

28 Prayer Services and
Activities for Children in K Through Sixth Grade

Patricia Mathson

9484

AVE MARIA PRESS
Notre Dame, Indiana 46556

International Standard Book Number: 0–87793–392–8

Library of Congress Catalog Card Number: 88–83549

Cover design: Elizabeth J. French

Printed and bound in the United States of America.

This book is dedicated to my children,
Cathy and Steve,
who have shown me God's love
and presence in the world.

Contents

Introduction

As a community of God's people we need to make prayer a priority in our classrooms, our churches, our homes and our lives. We need to be a people of prayer who acknowledge our dependence on God, Creator and Father. Ours is a God of love who calls us to share in his divine life through his Son, Jesus Christ. We should respond to that love with our lives and our prayers.

The prayer services in this book call children together to pray as the family of God. As children of God, our relationship with our Father necessarily involves the other people in his family. Children need the opportunity to explore their faith and their faith relationships.

The 28 prayer services are designed for children in kindergarten through sixth grade. They center on seasons and feasts in the church year and important days in the school year from September to May. Included are celebrations of various saints who have followed God's will in their lives and serve as examples to all of us. No one group is expected to participate in all these prayer services. Rather, carefully choose those most meaningful to the children in the group and those that fit the religious education program being used.

Each prayer service begins with the sign of the cross as an acknowledgment of our faith in God—Father, Son and Holy Spirit. It reminds us that all we do should be done for the glory of God.

The greeting sets the theme of the day's prayer service and serves as a welcome. This introduction tells the children why they are gathered together to celebrate.

Music is a joyful experience for children and a wonderful way to praise God. Its common language serves to unite them in prayer. Suggestions are given for children's songs appropriate to the theme of each prayer service. Other appropriate songs may be substituted. The Directory at the back of the book lists resources for music.

Some prayer services include an additional activity to help children participate more fully. Children learn by doing. It is important that they understand the theme being celebrated. These extra activities are another way to involve the children in prayer and praise of God.

Each prayer service centers on a scripture reading from the New Testament. The word of God in the Bible is important in our lives. God reveals himself to us through the Bible. We must know his word if we are to know who we are called to be as followers of Jesus Christ.

The reflection helps children more clearly understand the bible reading and the feast or season being celebrated. The reflections are meant to be a source of information as well as inspiration. They relate the bible reading to our lives today.

In the prayer response we ask for God's help in our lives. It carries out the theme of the feast or season. The prayer helps children learn to pray to God about all things. Children can also be encouraged to write their own petitions for some of the prayer services. The closing prayer provides a fitting conclusion to each prayer service and serves to focus thinking on the theme presented.

The final sign of the cross reminds us that everything we do should be done in God's name and with his help. It also signifies the conclusion to each prayer service.

Involve the children as much as possible in these prayer services. The older the children, the more they can make the prayer services their own by their participation. The majority of the readings should be done by the children themselves depending upon their ages and ability. As many children as possible should have the opportunity to read and lead prayers throughout the year if they choose to do so.

The area where the prayer services are held can help set the theme for each one. Display a Bible on a table at the front of the prayer area to stress the importance of the word of God. A silk plant, basket of flowers, or potted plant can signify our new life with God through his Son, Jesus. Banners and posters can reflect the theme of the special day and focus attention on what is being celebrated.

The enrichment ideas that follow each prayer service are meant to help children live the message of Christ in their lives. A variety of activities helps the children celebrate the joy of being people of God, learn about their faith or find ways to reach out to others. Select the ideas with the needs and interests of each class in mind.

This book is meant to help children learn to respond to God's presence in their hearts and lives. Being a Christian means being part of a faith community that expresses its faith through prayer to God, our Father and Creator. Sharing in prayer is a vital part of who we are as Christians.

*F*ollow Me

Beginning-of-year prayer service

Opening: In the name of the Father, and of the Son, and of the Holy Spirit. Amen.

Greeting: As we begin a new school year, let us remember to follow Jesus in all that we do.

Opening Song: "Come Along With Me to Jesus"(*Hi God 2*)

Bible Reading: This is a reading from the gospel of Mark (1:16–18):
   "As [Jesus] passed by the Sea of Galilee, he saw Simon and his brother Andrew casting their nets into the sea; they were fishermen. Jesus said to them 'Come after me; I will make you fishers of men.' Then they left their nets and followed him."

Reflection: In this reading Jesus called his first followers. Jesus calls each of us to follow him also. He teaches us by his life how we are to live as Christians. Being a Christian is more than a name, it is a way of life.
   We must answer the call of Jesus in our lives. We must live as witnesses to what he taught. We are called to follow him in faith, hope and love through everything we do.

Prayer Refrain: Now let us pray together.

> May we find joy in the year ahead. . .
> *Lord, hear our prayer*
>
> May we meet the challenges in our lives. . .
> *Lord, hear our prayer*
>
> May we see the good in all people. . .
> *Lord, hear our prayer*
>
> May we follow you always. . .
> *Lord, hear our prayer*

Song: "Follow Me" (*Celebrating God's Life*)

Closing Prayer:

Dear Jesus,
Open our minds and our hearts to your call in our lives.
Help us to learn more about you this year that we may love
you even more.
Be with us in all that we do so that we may truly be a
Christian people.

Response: In the name of the Father, and of the Son, and of the
Holy Spirit. Amen.

Enrichment Ideas

Mosaic Fish.   Children learn by doing and they like to be creative. To help them remember that Jesus calls us to follow him, children can make a mosaic fish. Remind the children that Jesus' first followers were fishermen.

Each child needs a sheet of blue construction paper to represent water. On the paper the children draw the outline of a large fish. Provide a posterboard pattern for those children who need it. At the bottom of the paper ask the children to print "Jesus calls his followers."

Children make mosaic tiles for their fish by cutting small squares from bright colors of construction paper. Red, orange, green and yellow make a colorful fish. The children glue the paper squares onto their fish in any arrangement they like. They can put a few squares on their fish or they can fill it with overlapping colors.

The children should be encouraged to use their imaginations so each fish is a unique creation. The fish can be taken home and displayed as a reminder that Jesus calls all of us to be fishers of people.

Echo Pantomime.   The story of Jesus calling his apostles can be retold by the teacher and children through an echo pantomime. The teacher says one line and does the accompanying motion. The children repeat the words and action like an echo.

One day Jesus was walking	(walk in place)
along the Sea of Galilee.	(make waves with hand)
He saw Peter and Andrew	(hand shades eyes)
fishing in their boat.	(pretend to row)
Jesus called to them	(hands cup mouth)
to come and follow him.	(beckon with arm)
Peter and Andrew said yes	(shake head up and down)
and left their boat to follow.	(walk in place)
Jesus also called others	(beckon with arm)

and they too said yes.	(shake head up and down)
The apostles followed Jesus	(walk in place)
as he told the good news.	(arms outstretched)
Today Jesus calls us	(beckon with arm)
to follow him.	(walk in place)
He wants us to care about others	(arms across chest)
and to tell people about him.	(arms outstretched)

The children will better remember the story and the message by being active participants.

Goal Essay.   Goal setting is important. It helps us direct our lives in a meaningful way. Ask the children at the beginning of the school year to write a short essay about one way they can answer Jesus' call in their lives. This offers children the opportunity and incentive to think about the coming year and how they can live the message of Jesus. Such a writing activity personalizes the idea of Jesus' call to follow him. Ask for only a paragraph or two. A long essay can quickly get discouraging for some children. The important idea is to think about the topic rather than fill the page. Encourage the children to concentrate on one main idea that they can actually carry through in their lives. This helps the children set an attainable goal for the year.

Saint From Assisi

St. Francis prayer service

Opening: In the name of the Father, and of the Son, and of the Holy Spirit. Amen.

Greeting: We honor St. Francis of Assisi each year on October 4. He was a joyful person who told people to trust in God.

Opening Song: "Peace Prayer" (*A Dwelling Place*)

Bible Reading: This reading is from the gospel of Matthew (19:21):
   "Jesus said to [the young man], 'If you wish to be perfect, go, sell what you have and give to [the] poor, and you will have treasure in heaven. Then come, follow me.'"

Reflection: St. Francis followed Jesus' words in this reading. He lived in the town of Assisi in Italy. When he was young, he lived the easy life of a wealthy merchant's son. Later he heard God's call in his life and gave away everything he had.
   St. Francis preached the good news about Jesus all over Italy. He saw the beauty in all God's creation. He had a special relationship with animals and talked to them as creatures of God. He lived the message of the gospel in his life every day.

Prayer Litany:

> St. Francis, preacher of the good news. . .
>   *Pray for us*
> St. Francis, friend of the poor. . .
>   *Pray for us*
> St. Francis, brother of all. . .
>   *Pray for us*
> St. Francis, helper of animals. . .
>   *Pray for us*
> St. Francis, follower of the gospel. . .
>   *Pray for us*

Closing Song: "The Blessing of St. Francis" (*Happy the Man* by Sebastian Temple)

Closing Prayer: Let us now pray the words of St. Francis:[1]

> You are holy, Lord, the only God,
>   and your deeds are wonderful.
> You are strong.
>   You are great.
>   You are the Most High,
>   You are almighty.
>   You, holy Father, are
>   King of heaven and earth.
> You are Three and One,
>   Lord God, all good.
>   You are Good, all Good, supreme Good,
>   Lord God, living and true.
> You are love.

Response: In the name of the Father, and of the Son, and of the Holy Spirit. Amen.

Enrichment Ideas

Bookmarks.   Give each child a St. Francis bookmark or holy card bearing a picture on the front and his famous peace prayer on the back. This will help children remember the example of St. Francis. They will also have the words of the prayer available to them at home. The bookmark will be a reminder of St. Francis and help extend the learning beyond the classroom.

Posters.   St. Francis led a very interesting life. Talk with the children about some of the fascinating details of this saint's life. Then ask them to draw posters showing various events. Scenes they might draw include the following:

> giving his cloak to a beggar
>
> fixing a church
>
> teaching people about God
>
> speaking to his followers
>
> organizing the first nativity scene
>
> talking to the animals

Children can work in pairs or alone. Provide posterboard and colorful markers. Place the completed posters along the hallway for all to see, in honor of St. Francis. Be sure each poster is marked with the name of the scene shown.

Paper Birds.   St. Francis loved animals. It is said that when he preached about God even the birds in the trees listened. Show the children how to make paper birds that can be hung on a potted tree branch.

Provide various colors of construction paper for the children. One half sheet of paper per child should be ample. Birds can be almost any color—blue (bluebirds), red (cardinals), white (doves), brown (robins), and yellow (canaries). Let the children choose which type of bird they want to make. Using a pattern, the children cut out the side view of a bird with a wide tail. Then the children cut out one piece pointed on either end and narrow in the middle to be the wings for the birds. The wing piece is pulled through a horizontal slit made in the middle of each bird. Then the piece is creased in the middle so that the wings point down. These three dimensional birds almost look ready to fly.

Give the children a hole punch so that they can put a hole in the top of their bird. A short piece of string can be threaded through and tied in a knot for a hanger. A dead tree branch can be potted to make a five-foot-tall tree. The short branches and twigs are good places for the children to hang their birds.

Heroes for Christ

All Saints Day prayer service

Opening: In the name of the Father, and of the Son, and of the Holy Spirit. Amen.

Greeting: This week on November 1 we will celebrate All Saints Day. It is a day to honor all people who have loved and served God. Today we will have the opportunity to think about saints and how they are examples for all of us.

Opening Song: "When the Saints Go Marching In" (*Joy Together*)

Bible Reading: This is a reading from the first letter of Paul to the Corinthians (12:4–7):
   "There are different kinds of spiritual gifts but the same Spirit; there are different forms of service but the same Lord; there are different workings but the same God who produces all of them in everyone. To each individual the manifestation of the Spirit is given for some benefit."

Reflection: This reading reminds us that each one of us has been given special talents and abilities by God. Each of us is different, but each of us is created with gifts that we can use to serve God and other people. The saints show us many different ways of following Jesus. God calls each of us to help others and work for the good of all people.

Saint Litany: We ask the saints to pray to God on our behalf.

> St. Peter, person of great faith. . .
>   *Pray for us*
> St. Mary, mother of Jesus. . .
>   *Pray for us*
> St. Francis, follower of the gospel. . .
>   *Pray for us*
> St. Thomas Aquinas, writer of books. . .
>   *Pray for us*

St. Vincent de Paul, helper of the poor. . .
   Pray for us
St. Elizabeth Ann Seton, teacher of children. . .
   Pray for us

Closing Song: "I Heard the Lord" (*Jesus and His Friends*)

Closing Prayer: God, help us to go forth today to use our gifts to help other people as the saints did. Hear our prayer, O God, Father and Creator. In the company of all your saints, may we praise your name today and always.

Response: In the name of the Father, and of the Son, and of the Holy Spirit. Amen.

Enrichment Ideas

Patron Saints. Everyone needs a special saint as a source of inspiration. Encourage the children to look up information on their patron saint or on a saint they admire. Provide books on saints that the children can use for reference and information. Help children to choose a saint. This could be the saint after whom they were named, the saint on whose feast day they were born, a saint with the same national heritage as they have, or a saint with interests similar to theirs.

Ask each child to write one paragraph on their saint and read it to the class. The reports should begin with the name of the saint and the day on which that saint is honored. Then the rest of the report can give a short summary of the life of that saint. This activity helps personalize the lives of the saints for children. The children also have the opportunity to learn from one another about a variety of saints.

Guessing Game. Having the children guess the identity of a saint from three clues is a good way to review a unit on saints.[2]

Prepare the clues before class. Be sure there are at least as many saints as children in the class. If the parish or school is named after a saint, be sure to include that saint. Sample clues are as follows:

> I lived in Nazareth.
> My cousin's name was Elizabeth.
> I was the mother of Jesus.
> Which saint am I? *(Mary)*

> I was a friend to God's creatures.
> I founded an order called the Franciscans.
> I lived in Assisi, Italy.
> Which saint am I? *(Francis of Assisi)*

> I was a fisherman.
> Jesus called me to follow him.
> I was the leader of the apostles.
> Which saint am I? *(Peter)*

> I worked with Italian families in New York.
> I established orphanages and schools.

I was the first U.S. citizen canonized.
Which saint am I? *(Frances Xavier Cabrini)*

I was a carpenter.
Mary was my wife.
Jesus was my foster son.
Which saint am I? *(Joseph)*

I was a Franciscan.
I preached God's message.
I am the patron of searchers for lost objects.
Which saint am I? *(Anthony of Padua)*

I am called a Doctor of the Church.
I wrote over 100 books.
My mother, Monica, prayed for me.
Which saint am I? *(Augustine)*

I joined the Carmelites.
I served God in daily life.
I am called the Little Flower.
Which saint am I? *(Therese of the Child Jesus)*

Children gather in a circle and take turns reading the sets of clues out loud. The other children try to guess the identity of the saint. If no one guesses correctly, the child with the clues gives the name of the saint. All the children should get a chance to read.

Helper for God

St. Frances Xavier Cabrini prayer service

Opening: In the name of the Father, and of the Son, and of the Holy Spirit. Amen.

Greeting: On November 13 each year we remember St. Frances Xavier Cabrini. She helped the poor, the orphans and the sick in the United States.

Opening Song: "Helping Hands" (*Celebrating God's Life*)

Bible Reading: This reading is from the gospel of Matthew (13:44-46):

"The kingdom of heaven is like a treasure buried in a field, which a person finds and hides again, and out of joy goes and sells all he has and buys that field. Again, the kingdom of heaven is like a merchant searching for fine pearls. When he finds a pearl of great price, he goes and sells all that he has and buys it."

Reflection: In this reading Jesus tells parables to show what the kingdom of God is like. The kingdom of God is here present among us through Jesus and it will be fulfilled at the end of time. We are to look for the kingdom of God in the world and to work for it. It is a treasure or a pearl worth everything we have. Jesus calls us to God's kingdom. He calls us to help make it a reality in the world.

St. Frances Xavier Cabrini heard this call. She worked to make God's kingdom present in the world. She was born in Italy and wanted to be a missionary to tell people about Jesus. She was sent to the United States to work among Italian people who had recently come to this country. She founded orphanages, schools and hospitals. She began an order called the Missionary Sisters of the Sacred Heart of Jesus. Her followers today still work in inner-city neighborhoods among impoverished people.

Prayer Response: Now let us pray for the coming of God's kingdom.

> May we live together in love. . .
> > *Your kingdom come*
> May we be a people of peace. . .
> > *Your kingdom come*
> May we care for one another. . .
> > *Your kingdom come*
> May we help those who need us. . .
> > *Your kingdom come*
> May we always direct our lives toward you. . .
> > *Your kingdom come*

Closing Song: "The Kingdom of God Is Coming" (*Jesus and His Friends*)

Closing Prayer:

> *Dear God,*
> *Help us to make your kingdom a reality in the world.*
> *Help us to live the gospel as Jesus taught us.*
> *Help us to remember that all things are possible through*
> > *you.*

Response: In the name of the Father, and of the Son, and of the Holy Spirit. Amen.

CHRIST UNITED METHODIST CHURCH
4488 POPLAR AVENUE
MEMPHIS, TENNESSEE 38117

Enrichment Ideas

Handprint Mural. Children need to remember that Jesus calls each of us to help others as did St. Frances Xavier Cabrini. A mural is a good learning activity to which all the children can contribute. A hand is an easily understood symbol of helping others.

Use a sheet of butcher paper to make a handprint mural for the class. In the center print the theme "We can help others." Use three colors of tempera paint for this mural. Put the paint in disposable pie pans for easy cleanup. Also have a bucket of water nearby for cleaning the paint off of children's hands.

Guide each of the children to place a hand palm down in a pan of tempera paint. The hand should immediately go onto the mural and then into the bucket of water. This way no paint will get on their clothing. Help one child at a time and let them choose the color paint they want for their handprint. Remind the children that their handprint on the mural is a sign of their willingness to help others.

This handprint mural can be displayed in the classroom as a reminder that Christians are called to help other people. If the classes are small, several classes can contribute to one mural for display in the hallway as a proclamation and a promise.

Situations. We are called to build the kingdom of God on earth in our everyday relationships with other people. Read the following situations to the students one at a time. Guide a discussion of possible responses that would help others. Stress that there is no one right answer, but many possible ideas.

One of your classmates is ill and missed school today. What can you do?

Your younger brother feels badly because he is the worst hitter on his baseball team. What can you do?

You see a parent with a stroller trying to get through the door into a store. What can you do?

A friend stayed overnight on a Saturday night. The next day he is still there while you are getting ready for Mass. What can you do?

You see a new student looking for a place to sit in the cafeteria. What can you do?

Your little sister wants someone to play with her. What can you do?

You've outgrown some of your clothes and no longer need them. What can you do?

An elderly neighbor is struggling to rake leaves. What can you do?

Someone in your group makes a joke about another person and hurts that person's feelings. What can you do?

These situations are good discussion starters. They help students see that God wants us to help other people in our daily lives. One person does make a difference. Each of us is called to live the kingdom of God.

We Give Thanks

Thanksgiving prayer service

Opening: In the name of the Father, and of the Son, and of the Holy Spirit. Amen.

Greeting: We gather together during the Thanksgiving season to give thanks to God, who is the source of all our blessings.

Opening Song: "Thank You Lord" (*Hi God*)

Bible Story: This is a story retold from the Bible (based on Luke 17:11–19):

One day as Jesus was walking, ten lepers called out to him. They asked Jesus to have pity on them. Jesus told the lepers to go and show themselves to the priest. On the way, they were healed. One of the lepers ran back to Jesus and thanked him. Jesus asked why only one person came back when all ten were cured. Then Jesus told the man to go on his way because he had faith.

Reflection: In this story only one person came back to Jesus to say thank you. We need to be like that one person. We should respond to God's love in our lives with praise and thanksgiving. We must remember the many gifts God has given to us and thank him by our prayers and our actions.

Food Offering: As a sign of thanksgiving to God and our willingness to share with others, we now bring forward our food gifts for those in need. (Children come forward in twos and place canned goods in baskets while "A Child's Thanksgiving" (*Joy Together*) plays in the background)

Prayer Response: Now let us together give thanks to our God.

> For all the colors of the rainbow. . .
>   *Thank you, God*
> For the food we eat each day. . .
>   *Thank you, God*

For the smell of flowers and pine trees. . .
Thank you, God
For the sound of music and laughter. . .
Thank you, God
For people who care. . .
Thank you, God
For all your creation. . .
Thank you, God

Closing Song: "All Your Gifts of Life" (*Hi God 2*)

Closing Prayer:

God, our Father and Creator,
We thank you for your many gifts.
We thank you for the world around us:
   for birds that sing in the morning light,
   for tall green trees, for blue sky overhead.
We thank you for the people who love us
   and for all people who help make this
   world a better place.
Hear our prayer of praise for all that you
   have made for love of us.

Response: In the name of the Father, and of the Son, and of the
Holy Spirit. Amen.

Enrichment Ideas

Thank You Letters.   Thanksgiving is a good time to thank God for his creation and his blessings in our lives. One way children can learn about thanking God is through writing thank you letters to him.

Encourage the children to think of the many things in their lives for which they can be thankful. Then ask them to write a short letter to God saying thank you to him. Explain to the children that God knows what is in our hearts, but it is also important to express it.

The letters can begin "Dear God." The children can write a few sentences of thanks. Then they can sign the letters with their names. A thank you letter turns out like this:

> Dear God,
> Thank you for my dog and my friends and my family.
> Thank you for the flowers and the trees.
>
> > Your friend,
> > Amy

These letters are written from the children's own experiences and thus are meaningful to them. The thank you letters help children reflect on God's presence in their lives.

Doorknob Sign.   A fun project with stickers for the Thanksgiving season is a doorknob sign.[3] Children cut out colorful pieces of construction paper 10″ long by 4 ½″ wide. A slit and a circle are cut into the top to allow the sign to be hung over a doorknob. On each sign the children print the words "Thanks be to God." Then they draw a zig zag border along the outside edge.

Provide stickers of things for which children can be thankful such as animals, flowers, leaves, hearts, people, and the like. Let each child choose six stickers to put on the doorknob sign. Then the children can take home their signs to remind them to give thanks to God for his many gifts. This is a good idea especially for younger children.

Basket Program. Along with giving thanks should go sharing what we have with others. One way to do this is to collect food for a Thanksgiving basket program. These programs are sponsored by various agencies who help the needy. They provide food for a traditional Thanksgiving dinner free or at a reduced cost.

These organizations ask for donations of canned goods from the local community in order to meet the needs of thousands of people. Items needed are sweet potatoes, green beans, cranberry sauce, stuffing mix, canned pumpkin, pie crust mix, chicken broth, coffee and tea. Check with the sponsoring organization for any special requirements. They normally supply the turkey for each family and deliver the baskets themselves.

A good way to collect the items needed is for each grade level to be responsible for collecting a certain item. For example, kindergarten could collect sweet potatoes, first grade would be responsible for green beans, and so on. Provide boxes clearly marked for the cans collected. Set the date far enough in advance to give the organization time to pack the baskets and deliver them before Thanksgiving Day. This is a great way to help make Thanksgiving special for others.

Friend of Children

St. Nicholas prayer service

Opening: In the name of the Father, and of the Son, and of the Holy Spirit. Amen.

Greeting: On December 6 we honor St. Nicholas. He is the patron saint of children everywhere. Even today children in some countries put out their shoes the night before in hopes of having them filled with goodies on his day.

Opening Song: "Happy the Heart" (*Hi God*)

Bible Story: This is a story retold from the Bible (based on Matthew 6:1-4):
     Jesus told the people not to do good acts just so other people would notice them. In that way they have already been rewarded with people's approval. Jesus said that instead we should do good things in secret and to serve God. He knows what we do and will reward us in heaven.

Reflection: St. Nicholas was a man who followed this idea and helped people in secret. He was a fourth-century bishop who gave away money to people in need.
     One story about St. Nicholas tells how he tossed a bag of gold coins into the window of a poor man's house three nights in a row. No one knew where the money came from since St. Nicholas was careful not to be seen. But the man rejoiced because now his daughters had enough money to get married.
     St. Nicholas cared about other people and shared with them. He was a special friend to children. We can follow the example of St. Nicholas and help others as Jesus calls us to do.

Prayer Response: Let us pray.

> For those who live the gospel message. . .
>   *Lord, hear our prayer*
> For those who seek God's will. . .
>   *Lord, hear our prayer*

For the poor in our community. . .
  Lord, hear our prayer
For those in need of assistance. . .
  Lord, hear our prayer
For all children everywhere. . .
  Lord, hear our prayer

Closing Song: "Living With Jesus" (*Living God's Word*)

Closing Prayer:

Good St. Nicholas, we honor you
  on this your holy feast day.

We rejoice that you are the patron saint
  for peoples of many lands.

Come, great-hearted saint,
  and be our patron and companion
  as we, once again, prepare our homes and
  hearts for the great feast of Christmas,
  the birth of the Eternal Blessing, Jesus
  Christ.

May these sweets, these candy canes,
  be a sign of Advent joy for us.

May these candy canes,
  shaped just like your Bishop's staff,
  be for us a sign of your benevolent care.

We rejoice that you are the holy bringer of
  gifts and that so many have been
  delighted through your great generosity.

Help us to be as generous of heart.[4]

Closing Note: All children are invited to take a candy cane from the basket upon leaving in celebration of St. Nicholas Day.

Response: In the name of the Father, and of the Son, and of the Holy Spirit. Amen.

Enrichment Ideas

Mitten Collection.   St. Nicholas gave gifts to those in need. He especially cared about children. We can encourage students to give to other children through a mitten collection. Children can understand this project. Talk with them about how chilly hands get in the winter and how cold their hands would be if they had to go to school every day without mittens. Explain to the children that some parents do not have enough money to buy mittens. This project helps children become aware of the needs of other people.

Send home notes with the children asking for their parents' help in providing mittens for underprivileged children. Stress to the children that this is a voluntary project. Decorate a collection box and mark it "Mitten Collection." Place it in a hallway or vestibule so that other students will not know if some children are not able to participate. This project helps children in need and enables students to become aware of how they can help others like St. Nicholas did.

Candy Cane Decorations.   Children can make candy cane decorations for the classroom in celebration of St. Nicholas. Provide white posterboard and a candy cane pattern. Children should cut out 16″ high candy canes.

Red construction paper can be used to cut out stripes for the candy canes. Each candy cane needs about five stripes, although some children may choose to put on more. The stripes should be glued onto the candy canes at an angle. Have a finished decoration available so that the children can see how it can look.

These decorations can be taped to windows to brighten up the classroom. Later the children can take home their candy canes to decorate for Christmas.

Patroness of the Americas

Our Lady of Guadalupe prayer service

Opening: In the name of the Father, and of the Son, and of the Holy Spirit. Amen.

Greeting: On December 12 we celebrate the feast of Our Lady of Guadalupe. It is a day to honor Mary as the patroness of the Americas.

Opening Song: "Hail Mary" (*Hi God 2*)

Bible Reading: This is a reading from the gospel of Luke (1:46–49):

"And Mary said:
'My soul proclaims the greatness of
   the Lord,
my spirit rejoices in God my savior,
For he has looked upon his handmaid's lowliness;
behold, from now on all ages will call me blessed.
The Mighty One has done great things for me, and holy is
   his name.'"

Reflection: This reading from the Bible is called the Magnificat. It shows Mary's faith in God. Mary continues to serve God even now.

   The story of Our Lady of Guadalupe took place in Mexico in the year 1531. The Spanish had conquered the Aztec Indians, but were having a difficult time converting them to Christianity.

   One day Our Lady appeared to an Indian convert named Juan Diego who was on his way to Mass. She asked him to tell the bishop to build a church on the hill where she was standing. Juan Diego went to the bishop, but the bishop wanted proof.

   Juan Diego went back to Our Lady and told her about the bishop's request. Mary told him to gather the roses that were blooming on the barren hillside where flowers never grew. Juan Diego did this and took the flowers to the bishop in his cloak.

   When Juan Diego opened his cloak in front of the bishop the

roses fell out and there on his cloak was an image of Mary clothed in a mantle of stars and surrounded by the rays of the sun.

The church was built and named the Basilica of Our Lady of Guadalupe. Soon Christianity spread rapidly among the Indians throughout Mexico. Even today the cloak with the miraculous image of Mary is displayed at that church. The image is undimmed by time. Mary's appearance reminds us that God loves all his people and is always with us.

Prayer Response: Now let us pray together.

> Mary, Our Lady of Guadalupe. . .
> > *Pray for us*
> Mary, Patroness of the Americas. . .
> > *Pray for us*
> Mary, Queen of heaven. . .
> > *Pray for us*
> *Mary, Mother of God. . .*
> > *Pray for us*

Closing Song: "My Soul Magnifies the Lord" (*Hi God 2*)

Closing Prayer:

> Mary, our Lady of Guadalupe,
> > we honor you as the mother of Jesus
> > and an example of faith.
> We join you in praise of God who has
> > done wondrous things for us and who
> > continues to love us with an unending love.
> Help us to follow God's will in our lives
> > as you did in yours.
> May we always remember that Jesus came
> > for all people, all nations, all cultures.
> We thank you for your intercession
> > and ask you to continue to pray for us
> > now and always.

Response: In the name of the Father, and of the Son, and of the Holy Spirit. Amen.

Enrichment Ideas

Drawing.   Encourage the children to visualize the scene of Mary appearing to Juan Diego. Ask them to draw a picture of the meeting and Juan Diego gathering roses from the hillside.

Provide colorful markers and white paper for this activity so that the children can express their ideas. Through drawing this story the children reflect on what occurred. Instruct the children to title their papers "Our Lady of Guadalupe." Write the spelling on the board for them to copy.

Children enjoy expressing their thoughts and ideas artistically. Drawing motivates children to learn and makes learning interesting. They will have a paper to take home that will remind them of what they have learned of this appearance of Our Lady.

Spanish.   Teach the children a few Spanish words and phrases that are used by children in Mexico:

buenos dias	good morning
buenas tardes	good afternoon
sí	yes
gracias	thanks
por favor	please
bueno	good
amigo	friend
niña	girl
niño	boy
uno	one
dos	two
tres	three

Learning another language helps children realize that children everywhere have similar ideas, hopes and dreams even if they express them somewhat differently. The more we learn about other cultures, the more we can understand that we are all members of God's family. Our differences should not be a barrier, but instead should enrich us all.

Fiesta. In honor of Mary's appearance in Mexico have a Mexican fiesta. Enlist parent help with this project. Serve Mexican food and snacks for the children to taste. Play Mexican mariachi music. Encourage any children who have clothing from this country to wear it on the day of the fiesta. Ask someone from Mexico to tell children about customs there.

Hang up a piñata filled with candy and let the children take turns striking it with a stick while blindfolded. When the piñata is finally broken, the children can share the candy that falls out. Help the children joyfully explore this and other customs from this country so that they will better appreciate the Mexican culture.

Time of Hope

First week of Advent prayer service

Opening: In the name of the Father, and of the Son, and of the Holy Spirit. Amen.

Greeting: This is the first week of the Advent season. Advent is the time before Christmas when we prepare our hearts for the coming of Jesus. We wait in joyful hope for Christmas.

Lighting of the Advent Wreath: The four candles on our Advent wreath symbolize the four weeks of Advent. Today we light one purple candle for the first week of Advent. (Light one candle.)

Opening Song: "Away in a Manger" (traditional)

Bible Reading: This is a reading from the letter of Paul to the Romans (15:13):
    "May the God of hope fill you with all joy and peace in believing, so that you may abound in hope by the power of the holy Spirit."

Reflection: As Paul tells us in this reading, God is the source of all our hope. He keeps his promises to us. He sent Jesus, his only Son, to us. We must be a people of hope as were the Israelites who waited thousands of years for Jesus. We must also share that hope in God with others during the Advent season and always.

Prayer Response: Dear God, we offer our petitions to you.

> Help us to remember the meaning of Advent. . .
> > *We wait in joyful hope*
> Help us to get ready to welcome you. . .
> > *We wait in joyful hope*
> Help us to be a people of hope to others. . .
> > *We wait in joyful hope*
> Help us to rejoice at the coming of Jesus. . .
> > *We wait in joyful hope*

Closing Song: "Silent Night" (traditional)

Closing Prayer: Dear God, all around us people are getting ready for Christmas. We eagerly wait for the coming of your Son, Jesus. Help us to get ready in our hearts to celebrate his coming into the world and into our lives. May Advent be a time of hope for all of us.

Response: In the name of the Father, and of the Son, and of the Holy Spirit. Amen.

Enrichment Ideas

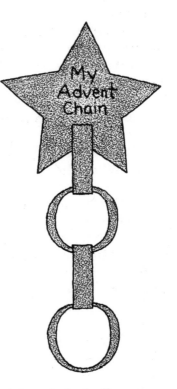

Star Chain.   A purple paper chain with four links can help children remember the four weeks of Advent. Each child needs a sheet of purple paper out of which to cut four 1″ wide strips and a large star with a tab at the bottom.

On each strip the children can print something they can do during Advent to get ready in their hearts for Jesus. Examples are: share my toys, say bedtime prayers, make Christmas cards for relatives, and help my family. The children will be able to think of other ideas suitable for their lives as the class discusses this project and the Advent season. The children tape the ends of one strip together to form a loop. The other strips are connected onto the one before to make a four-link chain.

On the large star the children print "My Advent chain." The points of the star can be decorated with self-stick stars. The chain is stapled onto the tab at the bottom of the star. Each week at home the children take off a link and do what is printed on the inside. This helps children learn that Advent is a special time to prepare for Jesus' coming at Christmas.

Family Day.   An interesting and enjoyable way to help families learn about Advent is a family activity day program.[5] Parish families with children of all ages are invited to a three hour program on a Sunday afternoon during Advent.

The program begins with prayer and ends with refreshments. In between families go to the classroom area where ten activity centers are set up. Someone is on hand in each room to explain the activity and answer questions. All materials are supplied. Families move from center to center, choosing activities suited to their interests and the ages of their children.

Activity centers include the following:

1. Banner making. Families make a small felt nativity banner to take home.

2. Coupons. Family members make coupons promising favors for one another as Christmas gifts.

3. Wrapping paper. Handmade wrapping paper is created which features red and green Christmas decorations.

4. Jesse tree. Patterns and explanations are provided so that families can make a paper tree with symbols representing Jesus' ancestors.

5. Candy cane game. Players walk around a circle in time to music. When the music stops, a number is drawn and the person standing on that number wins a candy cane.

6. Movie. Show an animated Christmas movie. (Movies can be rented free from the local public library.)

7. Nativity scene. Parents cut out paper nativity scenes and the children then color them.

8. Service. Parishioners make Christmas decorations for the local nursing home.

9. Ornaments. Families work together to make a Christmas tree ornament.

10. Book shop. Bibles, children's books, advent wreaths, and other items are made available for purchase.

This family day program gives families ideas about how they can celebrate Advent in their homes and gives them a way to spend an enjoyable afternoon learning together.

*T*ime of Light

Second week of Advent prayer service

Opening: In the name of the Father, and of the Son, and of the Holy Spirit. Amen.

Greeting: This is the second week of the Advent season. We wait for Jesus to come at Christmas. He is the light of the world, a light that all of us are to follow.

Lighting of the Advent Wreath: Today we light two purple candles for the second week of Advent. (Light two candles.) As Christmas grows closer, the light on our Advent wreath grows brighter.

Opening Song: "The First Noel" (traditional)

Bible Reading: This is a reading from the gospel of John (8:12):
  "Jesus spoke to [the people] again, saying 'I am the light of the world. Whoever follows me will not walk in darkness but will have the light of life.'"

Reflection: In this reading Jesus tells us that he is the light of our lives. We are to follow him as he has taught us. He will show us the way. We must let the light of Jesus shine in our lives.
  During this Advent season we should try to keep our focus on the light of Jesus. He is the reason we celebrate this holy season. We walk in his light.

Prayer Response: Let us pray.

> Help us always to follow you. . .
> *Jesus, you are the light of the world*
> Help those who walk in darkness. . .
> *Jesus, you are the light of the world*
> Help us to tell other people about you. . .
> *Jesus, you are the light of the world*
> Help us to prepare our lives for your coming. . .
> *Jesus, you are the light of the world*

Closing Song: "O Little Town of Bethlehem" (traditional)

Closing Prayer: Dear Jesus, you are the light of the world. Help us to follow you during this holy season of Advent and always. May we show forth your light in our lives so that others will come to know your love.

Response: In the name of the Father, and of the Son, and of the Holy Spirit. Amen.

Enrichment Ideas

Advent Wreath.   Children can make individual paper Advent wreaths to take home as a reminder of the season. Each child needs a sheet of light purple construction paper for the background. The children then cut out green wreaths following a pattern. Each child glues a wreath onto the background sheet. Then they cut out one pink and three dark purple candles and glue them onto each wreath.

The final step is to cut out two yellow flames and glue them over two of the purple candles. This lights the wreaths for the second week of Advent. This is a good way to help children remember the four weeks of Advent. The lit candles also symbolize that Jesus should be the light of our lives.

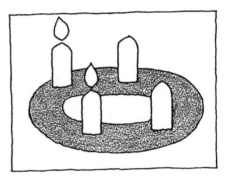

Stand-up Tree.   A simple gift children can make during Advent is a green paper tree. The children cut out two large tree shapes from sheets of green construction paper. The trees can have scalloped edges that get smaller near the top of the tree. The bottom of the tree should have a trunk. The trees can be about 9″ tall by 10″ wide.

The two trees are stapled together down the middle. Then the children fold the edges together and make a crease in the middle so that the tree will stand up by itself.

The children can decorate their trees with large self-stick stars. Remind the children that we put stars on Christmas trees to remind us of the star that shone over the stable in Bethlehem when Jesus was born. These trees make lovely Christmas gifts for the children to give to their parents. Each green tree is a gift from the heart and can stand on a bookshelf or piano at home.

(See following page for illustration)

Time of Joy

Third week of Advent prayer service

Opening: In the name of the Father, and of the Son, and of the Holy Spirit. Amen.

Greeting: This is the third week of Advent. It is a time of joy because Christmas is coming closer.

Lighting of the Advent Wreath: Today we light two purple candles and one pink candle to symbolize joy. (Light candles.)

Opening Song: "O Come All Ye Faithful" (traditional)

Bible Reading: This is a reading from the letter of Paul to the Colossians (3:16–17):
  "Let the word of Christ dwell in you richly, as in all wisdom you teach and admonish one another, singing psalms, hymns, and spiritual songs with gratitude in your hearts to God. And whatever you do, in word or in deed, do everything in the name of the Lord Jesus, giving thanks to God the Father through him."

Reflection: In this reading Paul reminds us that we should do everything in the name of Jesus. We are to be a joyful people because we have heard the good news. We must give thanks to God for sending Jesus to us.
  Everywhere we see signs of people getting ready to celebrate Christmas. Trees are decorated, gifts are wrapped and cards are sent. Let us remember that we do these things because we are filled with joy at the coming of Jesus into the world.

Prayer Response: Together we proclaim our joy.

Christmas is coming. . .
  We rejoice in the Lord
God has sent us his Son. . .
  We rejoice in the Lord

Jesus shows us the way. . .
We rejoice in the Lord
He calls us to follow him. . .
We rejoice in the Lord
We ask his help in all that we do. . .
We rejoice in the Lord

Closing Song: "Joy to the World" (traditional)

Closing Prayer: Dear God, we are filled with joy at the coming of Jesus. Help us to follow him and to live his message in our lives for the good of all people.

Response: In the name of the Father, and of the Son, and of the Holy Spirit. Amen.

Enrichment Ideas

Advent Poem.   Children can write their own personal poems about the meaning of Advent using the cinquain form:

> Line 1: One word title
> Line 2: Two descriptive words
> Line 3: Three action words
> Line 4: Four descriptive words
> Line 5: One word summary

To write a poem, each child has to reflect on the meaning of the Advent season for Christians. Such a poem turns out like this:

> Advent
> hopeful anticipation
> sharing, caring, helping,
> time of great love
> joy

These poems speak to the children of the personal meaning of the Advent season in their lives. They help children remember that we celebrate Advent as a special time to get ready for the coming of Jesus at Christmas.

Supply Tree.   Advent should be a time when we joyfully give to others. Help children to do this by collecting school supplies. Local charities get many requests for school supplies from families who are having a difficult time financially.

Send home notes explaining this Advent project and also tell the children about it. Lists of the most needed school supplies can be obtained from the local school district office or from the principal. Supplies most in demand include:

rulers	glue
pencils	pens
crayons	folders
notebook paper	construction paper
scissors	erasers
map pencils	binders

Set up an artificial Christmas tree in the vestibule or cafeteria. Hang lightweight donated items such as rulers, packages of pencils, crayons and scissors from the branches with red yarn.

Place brightly wrapped cartons under the tree for extra items and the heavier ones such as notebook paper. Arrange for delivery of the school supplies to the charity for distribution. This project benefits needy children and helps all children understand sharing with others.

Time of Love

Fourth week of Advent prayer service

Opening: In the name of the Father, and of the Son, and of the Holy Spirit. Amen.

Greeting: This is the fourth week of Advent. It is a time to share the love that Jesus brought us with others.

Lighting of the Advent Wreath: Today we light all four candles on our Advent wreath. (Light four candles.) Christmas is coming soon.

Opening Song: "It Came Upon the Midnight Clear" (traditional)

Bible Reading: This is a reading from the first letter of John (4:9):
      "In this way the love of God was revealed to us: God sent his only Son into the world that we might have life through him."

Reflection: This reading reminds us of God's great love for us. He loved us so much that he sent his only Son to us. Jesus showed God's love for us through all his words and actions.
      We must open our hearts and our lives to the love of God. We must show God our love for him and for all his people. We are called to be a community bonded together by God's love for us and by our love for one another.

Prayer Response: Let us pray.

> Help us to know God's love. . .
>   *Come, Lord Jesus*
> Help us to show that love to others. . .
>   *Come, Lord Jesus*
> Help us to be a caring people. . .
>   *Come, Lord Jesus*
> Help us to praise God in our lives. . .
>   *Come, Lord Jesus*

Closing Song: "Hark the Herald Angels Sing" (traditional)

Closing Prayer: Come, Lord Jesus, into our hearts and our lives this Advent season. Fill us with your love. As we prepare for your coming, help us to remember those who are in need. Show us the way to love all people in your name.

Response: In the name of the Father, and of the Son, and of the Holy Spirit. Amen.

Enrichment Ideas

Action Rhyme. An Advent action rhyme helps younger children understand what it is that we celebrate during this time. The motions help express the words.[6]

Let's count the days till Christmas   (count on fingers)
and say a prayer each day   (fold hands in prayer)
to show our love for Jesus   (hands on heart)
in a special way.   (nod head)

Jesus was born on Christmas   (rock arms)
and everyone should know   (point to others)
that Jesus came to save us   (open arms wide)
because he loves us so.   (hug self)

Jesus taught us to love   (hand on heart)
and how to share.   (nod head)
During this Advent time   (count on fingers)
let's show others we care.   (open arms wide)

This action rhyme helps children see the Advent season as a time of love and sharing with others.

Birthday Cards. Encourage the children to make birthday cards for Jesus. This helps younger children see Christmas as the celebration of Jesus' birthday in the midst of all the decorations and preparations.

Provide manila paper that the children can fold in half to make cards. Also have on hand various colors of markers with which the children can decorate their cards. Suggest that they make a design on the front such as a birthday cake or Christmas symbol. On the inside the child should print "Happy Birthday, Jesus" and sign his or her name. Display the cards in the classroom as a reminder that we celebrate Jesus' birthday each Christmas.

Tissue Wreath.   A simple, but lovely decoration that children can make is a wreath of tissue paper. Each child cuts out an 8″ diameter circle from green poster board. Then they cut away the inside leaving only a ring. This can be done ahead of time for younger children.

Provide green tissue paper that the children can cut into 3″ squares. Each square is gathered in the middle and pinched together. Then the gathered piece is glued onto the poster board ring. This continues until each child has a ring covered with green tissue.

This project produces beautiful three-dimensional wreaths handmade with love by the children for their families. The children feel a sense of accomplishment that they can contribute to decorating their homes for Christmas. The wreath can be displayed at home using double stick tape. The tissue wreaths brighten homes and hearts during the Advent season.

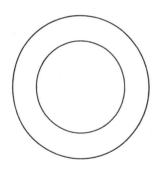 

God's Greatest Gift

Christmas prayer service

Opening: In the name of the Father, and of the Son, and of the Holy Spirit. Amen.

Greeting: We gather today to celebrate the great feast of Christmas which is fast approaching. God has given us the greatest gift of all, his Son. We rejoice at the coming of Jesus into the world and into our lives.

Bible Story Choral Reading:[7]

(Group 1)   This Christmas time we worship
　　　　　　as we gather here tonight
　　　　　　to welcome Lord Jesus
　　　　　　who came to bring us light.

　　(Children sing "O Little Town of Bethlehem")

(Group 2)   We worship as did Mary and Joseph
　　　　　　who by the manger stood.
　　　　　　They looked at Mary's holy Son
　　　　　　and knew that God was good.

　　(Children sing "Silent Night")

(Group 1)   We worship as did the angels
　　　　　　who sang the first Noel.
　　　　　　God had sent his only Son
　　　　　　good tidings did they tell.

　　(Children sing "The First Noel")

(Group 2)   We worship as did the shepherds
　　　　　　who came from hills so bare.
　　　　　　They brought with them little lambs
　　　　　　and saw Jesus lying there.

　　(Children sing "Away in a Manger")

(Both groups)   To Jesus, Lord and Savior,
we bring ourselves this night.
We worship and adore him
who brought us peace and light.

(All sing "Joy to the World")

Prayer Response: Let us pray together.

We rejoice at your coming. . .
Happy Birthday, Jesus
We praise your name among all people. . .
Happy Birthday, Jesus
We are people of joy and hope. . .
Happy Birthday, Jesus
We are people who care in your name. . .
Happy Birthday, Jesus

Closing Prayer:

Dear Jesus, we are full of joy
as we celebrate your birthday.
Help us to live our lives
so that we reflect that joy
during this holy season
and throughout the year.
Enable us to share with others the hope and
love you bring.

Response: In the name of the Father, and of the Son, and of the
Holy Spirit. Amen.

Enrichment Ideas

Christmas Bingo.   Children like to celebrate Christmas with the traditional class Christmas party. One game they might play on this day is Christmas bingo. This game uses words from the biblical account of the first Christmas. The words are printed inside 16 squares on each child's bingo card. Bingo cards can be made from 8½″ square pieces of paper. Use a pen and ruler to mark the squares. The words must be put in different order on the cards so that each card is different. The words for Christmas bingo are:

census	flocks
Mary	angel
Joseph	savior
Bethlehem	God
Nazareth	glory
son	joy
manger	Messiah
shepherds	baby

The words are called out from a master list. The children can mark their words with unpopped popcorn until one child gets four words in a row vertically, horizontally, or diagonally. This game can be played again and again.

savior	God	flocks	joy
baby	census	glory	Mary
angel	Messiah	Joseph	Shepherds
son	Nazareth	manger	Bethlehem

Burlap Banner.   Christmas should be a time to proclaim joy at the coming of Jesus. Children can make Christmas banners to give as gifts of joy to their families. Burlap and felt can be used to make beautiful individual banners. Each child needs a piece of burlap about 14″ long by 9″ wide with a rod pocket sewn in the top. Outside help should be enlisted to cut out the burlap from the rolls and sew the line of stitching across the top. Beige burlap provides a neutral background for the banners.

Red and green felt can be used for banner symbols and letters. Provide patterns for the children. Each child should cut out red or green letters to spell "JOY" and glue them diagonally in the middle of the banner. Then the children should choose two Christmas shapes for decoration. Good symbols are a bell, a candle, holly, a star, a gift, a tree, a wreath, or an angel. These should be cut out of the opposite color as the letters. One symbol can be glued in the upper right corner of the banner and the other in the lower left corner. Trim such as a bow on the bell or a flame on the candle should be the same color as the letters.

Last the children put a 10″ wooden dowel through the pocket in the top of the banner. An 18″ piece of red or green yarn tied to the ends of the dowel makes the banner ready for hanging. This is a gift made with love that lasts year after year. It proclaims joy to all who see it.

*F*ollowing the Star

Epiphany prayer service

Opening: In the name of the Father, and of the Son, and of the Holy Spirit. Amen.

Greeting: This week we will celebrate the feast of Epiphany. We remember the wise men who travelled from afar to find Jesus and give him gifts.

Opening Song: "What Child Is This" (traditional)

Bible Story: This is a story retold from the Bible (based on Matthew 2:1–12).

After Jesus was born, wise men from the east saw a bright star in the sky. They knew that something special had happened. They followed the star until they came to where Jesus was. They honored Jesus and gave him gifts of gold, frankincense and myrrh.

Reflection: In this story we heard about the wise men who searched for Jesus. The feast of Epiphany offers us the opportunity to think about what Jesus means to us. Like the wise men, we should look for his star in our lives and follow it. Like them we too must bring him gifts, especially the gift of our hearts and our love.

This story is important also because it helps us remember that Jesus came for people of all nations, near and far. He came because God loves all of us.

Prayer Response: We ask the Lord to be with us in all things.

> May we look for your star in our lives. . .
>   *Be with us, Lord*
> May we follow you in all that we do. . .
>   *Be with us, Lord*
> May we give you the gift of our love. . .
>   *Be with us Lord*

May we share the good news with others. . .
Be with us, Lord

Closing Song: "We Three Kings of Orient Are" (traditional)

Closing Prayer: Help us, Lord, on this feast of Epiphany to follow your star. Thank you for coming to show us the way to the Father. Help us to serve you with willing hearts in all that we do.

Response: In the name of the Father, and of the Son, and of the Holy Spirit. Amen.

Enrichment Ideas

Mosaic Star. This craft project helps children remember the story of the wise men. On a sheet of yellow construction paper have each child trace the outline of a large star using a pattern. Provide other colors of construction paper such as blue, green, purple, orange and red. Tell the children to cut out small squares from the colored paper. Squares can be approximately one inch square, but may vary in size.

Follow the star

The children glue the paper squares inside their star outline in a random arrangement. Squares should overlap one another, but the entire star need not be covered. The stars can be as individual as the children choose to make them by the pattern of colors and the number of paper squares used. Have the children print "Follow the star" at the bottom of the page.

This mosaic star turns out to be bright and colorful. The children are pleased and proud to take home these stars as a reminder to follow Jesus in their lives.

Epiphany Play. A play about the journey of the wise men can be presented by older students for younger grades. This becomes a learning activity for both groups. A play such as "The Epiphany" from *Child's Play* (see the Directory) is a dramatic presentation based on Matthew's account of the wise men's search for Jesus. A narrator in the play tells the audience about the meaning of the story so that the children will understand that Jesus came for all people.

In this play there are only a few lines to learn so preparation time is minimal. Directions for staging and simple props are given. If all the children wear nametags identifying their characters the play is easy for the audience to follow. A play makes the story from the Bible come alive for children.

American-Born Saint

St. Elizabeth Ann Seton prayer service

Opening: In the name of the Father, and of the Son, and of the Holy Spirit. Amen.

Greeting: On January 4 we honor St. Elizabeth Ann Seton. She was the first American-born saint canonized.

Opening Song: "Children of the Lord" (*Jesus and His Friends*)

Bible Story: This is a story retold from the Bible (based on Mark 10:13-16):

One day Jesus was teaching the people. Some parents brought their little children up to Jesus. The disciples told them to go away. But Jesus said, "Let the children come to me." Then he blessed them because Jesus came for all people.

Reflection: In this story Jesus shows that he cares about children. A saint who cared about children was St. Elizabeth Ann Seton. She was a widow with five children who became a Catholic. This caused trouble with her friends who didn't understand. She followed Jesus and lived the gospel every day even when it wasn't easy. Elizabeth Ann Seton was a teacher and she founded the first parochial school in the United States. She wanted children to learn about God too.

Prayer Response: Let us pray.

> May we seek your will in all things. . .
>   *Lord, guide us*
> May we live our lives as your followers. . .
>   *Lord, guide us*
> May we see you in all people. . .
>   *Lord, guide us*
> May we teach others about you. . .
>   *Lord, guide us*

Closing Song: "Living and Loving and Learning" (*Hi God 3*)

Closing Prayer: Dear God, we ask you to watch over us and guide us. Help us always to remember your love and your care.

Response: In the name of the Father, and of the Son, and of the Holy Spirit. Amen.

Enrichment Ideas

Verse Chain.   Children can make a verse chain to help them remember that Jesus cares about them. Each link of this paper chain contains one word to spell out "Let the children come to me." These were Jesus' words in the story of Jesus and the children.

Children need six different colors of paper to make this chain. It is easiest to cut the paper ahead of time with a paper cutter into 1" wide strips. Put the strips into separate boxes by color so that the children can easily get one of every color. The children write one word on each color paper. For example, "Let" would be printed on a red paper strip, "the" would be printed on blue, and so on.

The children then assemble the paper chain in order by taping the ends of one strip together and linking another through it. Be sure that they get the words in the correct order beginning with "Let" and ending with "me." Making this chain helps the children become familiar with the words of Jesus and remember that Jesus loves them. When they have finished, each child will have a verse chain to take home at the end of class.

Echo Pantomime.   An echo pantomime allows children to participate in the retelling of the story of Jesus and the children. The teacher says one line and does the action. The children repeat the words and motions. Each line follows another in this way.

One day Jesus was speaking	(hands cup mouth)
to great crowds who followed him.	(beckon with arm)
Some children came also	(hand few feet off ground)
to see and hear Jesus teach.	(shade eyes with hand)
The disciples said, "Go away,	(pushing motion with hands)
Jesus is very busy today."	(shake finger)
But Jesus told the disciples,	(hands cup mouth)
Let the children come to me,	(beckon with arm)
I love them one and all.	(hug self)
Then the children ran to him;	(run in place)

they knew that Jesus cared.   (nod head)
Jesus blessed each one of them   (place hand on head)
and sent them on their way.   (wave goodbye)
Jesus loves all people now   (hug self)
Just as he did back then.   (nod head)
He calls us to come to him   (beckon with arm)
you and you and you and me   (point to others, then self)
for he loves us one and all.   (arms open wide)

Blessing of Throats

St. Blase prayer service

Opening: In the name of the Father, and of the Son, and of the Holy Spirit. Amen.

Greeting: On February 3 we celebrate the feast of St. Blase. It is a tradition that each year we ask for his blessing against ailments of the throat.

Opening Song: "Celebrate God" (*Hi God*)

Bible Reading: This is a reading from the gospel of Matthew (4:23):
"[Jesus] went around all of Galilee, teaching in their synagogues, proclaiming the gospel of the kingdom, and curing every disease and illness among the people."

Reflection: Jesus came to teach people about the good news. He also healed people as a sign that God's kingdom was here present among us through Jesus.
Some saints have been given the ability to heal people in Jesus' name. One such saint was Saint Blase. A legend about him says that one day a woman came up to him with her son in her arms. The child had a fishbone caught in his throat and was choking. At Blase's command the child was able to cough up the bone and his life was saved. So now we ask the blessing of St. Blase too.

Blessing: All present are now invited to come forward and receive the blessing of St. Blase for their throats. (If possible a priest or deacon should administer this blessing.)
Holding two crossed candles in front of each person's throat, say: "Through the intercession of St. Blase, bishop and martyr, may God deliver you from all ailments of the throat and from every other illness. In the name of the Father, and of the Son, and of the Holy Spirit. Amen."

Prayer Response: Now let us pray to the Lord.

For doctors, nurses and chaplains who help the sick. . .
   Lord, hear our prayer
For those in hospitals or having surgery. . .
   Lord, hear our prayer
For elderly people confined to nursing homes. . .
   Lord, hear our prayer
For people suffering from mental illness or depression. . .
   Lord, hear our prayer
For all people who are sick or burdened with great cares. . .
   Lord, hear our prayer

Closing Song: "Wherever I Am, God Is" (*Hi God 3*)

Closing Prayer: Dear God, help us to remember your love and care in times of illness. We know that you are always with us. Help us to minister to the sick with kindness and bring them the good news of your love for all people.

Response: In the name of the Father, and of the Son, and of the Holy Spirit. Amen.

Enrichment Ideas

Get Well Card.   Encourage the children to make get well cards for a sick classmate or teacher.[8] Talk with the children about how it feels to be sick. Children are usually eager to participate in such a discussion. Explain that get well cards show sick people that others care and are thinking about them.

Each card should be handmade by the giver as a wish from the heart. Give some direction to those who need it such as making a cartoon on the front with a get well message. Another idea is to print a rhyme on the inside such as "Roses are red, violets are blue. Get well quick, we miss you." But mainly encourage the children to use their own creative abilities. The individuality of the cards is much of their charm.

When all the children are finished, collect the cards in a large manila envelope and see that they are delivered to the person who is ill. If a thank you note is received for the cards, be sure to read it to the class the next time they meet.

Gift-a-day.   In this outreach project for a child facing a serious illness or injury, the children provide a gift to open each day of recuperation. Send home notes with the children explaining the situation and asking parents to help. Each child who wants to participate can bring a small gift. Appropriate gifts for sick children are books, one-player games, crossword puzzle books, comic books, drawing paper, special interest magazines, a small stuffed animal and the like.

Make tags with the names of the days of the week. Have each child pick one and tape it on top of the gift he or she is giving. This is the day on which this gift should be opened by the recipient. In a large class the gifts can be marked morning or afternoon too.

This project helps brighten the days for a sick child who is unable to attend school or church functions with the other children. It spreads out the enjoyment and gives the child something to do and something to anticipate. Be sure to include a note explaining the idea in the box of gifts. This project helps children help one another.

Sharing God's Love

St. Valentine's Day prayer service

Opening: In the name of the Father, and of the Son, and of the Holy Spirit. Amen.

Greeting: We will soon celebrate St. Valentine's Day. Although there was a St. Valentine many years ago, we do not know much about him or how the holiday actually started. But we can see this day as a special time to remember God's love for us and how we are to share it with others.

Opening Song: "God Has Made Us a Family" (*Hi God 3*)

Bible Reading: This is a reading from the gospel of Matthew (22:35-40):
   "One of them [a scholar of the law] tested [Jesus] by asking, 'Teacher, which commandment of the law is the greatest?' [Jesus] said to him: 'You shall love the Lord, your God, with all your heart, with all your soul, and with all your mind. This is the greatest and first commandment. The second is like it: You shall love your neighbor as yourself. The whole law and the prophets depend on these two commandments.' "

Reflection: In this reading Jesus tells the people that they must love God with everything they have. This is to be our response to God's unending love for us. He freely gives his love to us and will continue to love us always.
   Jesus tells us to love other people. We are to share the wonderful gift of God's love with others. We must be a people of God who show forth love in everything we do. Only then do we live the way Jesus taught.

Heart Tree: As a sign that we will follow Jesus in loving others, each person may come forward to place a name heart on our tree. (Children put paper hearts on a posterboard tree with double stick tape. The song "That's the Way It Was Meant to Be" (*Jesus and His Friends*) plays in the background.)

Prayer Response: Now let us together thank God.

> For your unending love for us. . .
> > *We thank you, God*
> For the love of our families and friends. . .
> > *We thank you, God*
> For our parish community. . .
> > *We thank you God*
> For those who share their time and talents. . .
> > *We thank you, God*
> For people who make this world a bettter place. . .
> > *We thank you, God*
> For sending Jesus to teach us. . .
> > *We thank you, God*

Closing Song: "What Makes Love Grow" (*Hi God*)

Closing Prayer:

> Dear Jesus,
> You told us to love others as ourselves.
> Help us to see you in the people we meet,
> > especially the lonely, the poor and the sick.
> May we bring them the light of your love
> > so they will know that we care.

Response: In the name of the Father, and of the Son, and of the Holy Spirit. Amen.

Enrichment Ideas

Wax Paper Heart.   A multicolored heart can be a reminder to children that they are to love God and love others in his name. This heart is made from wax paper and tissue paper to produce a stained glass effect.

Each child needs two sheets of wax paper. The children cut through both sheets at once to form two heart shapes of the same size. Provide a pattern for the children of a 7″ heart.

For the stained glass effect use bright colors of tissue paper such as red, blue and green. The children cut the tissue paper into pieces about 1″ square. The squares do not need to be uniform size. Then let the children use glue sticks to glue the tissue squares onto one of the wax paper hearts in an overlapping design. Next they lay the other wax paper heart on top.

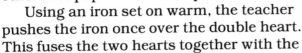

Using an iron set on warm, the teacher pushes the iron once over the double heart. This fuses the two hearts together with the tissue squares in between. A table-top ironing board is safest for this project.

Instruct the children to each put his or her name along one edge of the heart with a black permanent marker so that it can later be identified. The hearts can be displayed using double stick tape in a sunny window. The array of colorful hearts speaks to the children of love.

God Loves Us All Action Rhyme.   Children need to feel God's love in their lives. The following action rhyme helps them to know that God cares about each one of them.[9]

Some people are big,	(stand on tiptoes)
some people are small	(stoop)
but it doesn't matter	(shake head)
for God loves us all.	(hug self)
Some people are loud	(hands cup mouth)
some people are shy,	(finger over mouth)
but God loves all people	(smile)
and I'll tell you why.	(nod head)

All people need love	(extend arms wide)
and someone who'll hear	(cup hand behind ear)
their prayers and their praises	(fold hands)
and always be near	(nod head)
We thank you, dear God,	(fold hands)
for your love and care.	(hug self)
Help us to love others	(hand on heart)
and learn how to share.	(arms outstretched)

This type of action rhyme helps children remember God's love and reminds them to share that love with others.

Missionary to Ireland

St. Patrick's Day prayer service

Opening: In the name of the Father, and of the Son, and of the Holy Spirit. Amen.

Greeting: We celebrate St. Patrick's Day on March 17. St. Patrick told the people of Ireland the good news about Jesus.

Opening Song: "I Will Be With You" (*Jesus and His Friends*)

Bible Reading: This reading is from the gospel of Matthew (28:18-20):
   "Then Jesus approached [the disciples] and said to them, 'All power in heaven and on earth has been given to me. Go, therefore, and make disciples of all nations, baptizing them in the name of the Father, and of the Son, and of the holy Spirit, teaching them to observe all that I have commanded you. And behold, I am with you always, until the end of the age.' "

Reflection: In this reading Jesus tells his followers to teach other people and baptize them. One person who did this was St. Patrick. He used shamrocks to show people that there was one God, but three persons, Father, Son and Holy Spirit. He travelled all over Ireland teaching people about Jesus, baptizing them, and building churches. He was a missionary with faith in God who wanted to share that faith with other people.

Prayer Response: We now ask the Lord to hear us.

   We pray that everyone will hear the good news. . .
      Lord, hear our prayer
   We pray for missionaries here and far away. . .
      Lord, hear our prayer
   We pray for all those who teach others about Jesus. . .
      Lord, hear our prayer
   We pray that we too may serve God in our lives. . .
      Lord, hear our prayer

73

Closing Song: "Our God Is a God of Love" (*Hi God 2*)

Closing Prayer: Let us pray the words of St. Patrick:

> Christ shield me this day:
> Christ with me, Christ before me,
> Christ behind me, Christ within me,
> Christ beneath me, Christ above me,
> Christ on my right, Christ on my left,
> Christ when I lie down, Christ when I arise.
> Christ in the heart of everyone who thinks of me,
> Christ in the mouth of everyone who speaks of me,
> Christ in every eye that sees me,
> Christ in every ear that hears me.

Response: In the name of the Father who created us, the Son who redeemed us, and the Holy Spirit who lives in us. Amen.

Enrichment Ideas

Greeting Card.   Each child in the class can make a greeting card for a family member or friend to wish them a happy St. Patrick's Day. Talk with the children about who might be especially pleased to receive such a card —a parent, grandparent, neighbor and so on.

Sheets of light and dark green construction paper can be folded in half for cards. Some children will want to trim some paper off the bottom to make a square card. Then the children cut out shamrocks for decorations for the front of their cards. Light green shamrocks look good on dark green cards and dark green shamrocks look good on light green cards. Provide patterns of large and small shamrocks so that the children can choose the size and number of shamrocks they want to cut out for their card.

Shamrock stickers can be purchased at card shops and add an extra special touch to the cards. Remind the children to print "Happy St. Patrick's Day" on the inside and sign their cards. Greeting cards are a good way for children to share the joy of this day with other people in their lives.

Shamrock Border.   Let the children decorate their classroom with a border of shamrocks in honor of St. Patrick's Day. This is simple to do. Cut pieces of green paper into strips four inches wide. Show the children how to fold the paper strips in an accordion fold. Then they cut a shamrock shape out of the folded paper through several thicknesses at once.

When the paper is unfolded a row of shamrocks emerges connected together at the sides. The children can connect several strips of shamrocks together with tape until a border of the desired length is reached. This bright border can be used to edge the bulletin board or put around a door or window in the classroom.

Party Placemat.   St. Patrick proclaimed the good news about Jesus to the people of Ireland. Celebrate this saint's day with a party in his honor. Let the children each make a placemat for the party. A placemat can be made easily from a sheet of construction paper. Let the children cut out shamrocks to glue onto their placemats. Then show them how to fringe the edge by making 1/2" deep cuts with a scissors all around. Lime drink and shamrock cookies with green icing can be provided by parents and served at the party by older students. Green balloons and party streamers can be used to complete the party decorations.

Time of Growth

First week of Lent prayer service

Opening: In the name of the Father, and of the Son, and of the Holy Spirit. Amen.

Greeting: This is the first week of the Lenten season. Lent is a time when we should grow in faith and love of God. It is a time of renewal that helps us prepare to celebrate the great feast of Easter.

Opening Song: "Listen, Listen" (*Hi God*)

Bible Reading: This is a reading from the gospel of John (14:23):
    "Whoever loves me will keep my word, and my Father will love him, and we will come to him and make our dwelling with him."

Reflection: In this reading Jesus talks of how we are to be true to his word. Jesus is the word of God who reveals the Father to us. We are to follow God's word in Jesus and then God's love will live in our hearts. As Christians we are called to be faithful to the word of God. During this season of Lent let us strive to learn about the word of God and let it grow in our lives.

Prayer Response: We now ask Jesus to help us.

> Jesus, light of the world. . .
>   *Guide our lives*
> Jesus, the bread of life. . .
>   *Strengthen us*
> Jesus, the way, the truth, and the life. . .
>   *Hear our prayers*
> Jesus, the word of God. . .
>   *Teach us to follow you*

Song: "Speak, O Lord" (Celebrating God's Life)

Closing Prayer:

Dear God,
Let your word grow in our lives
    during this holy season of Lent.
Help us to be people of your kingdom who
    spread the word of God to others.
Direct our lives so that we do everything in
    your name.

Response: In the name of the Father, and of the Son, and of the Holy Spirit. Amen.

Enrichment Ideas

Matching Game. In order to follow Jesus we need to know what he calls us to do. A matching game helps children become familiar with the words of Jesus in the Bible.

To make this game cut eight unlined index cards in half. Print the words of each verse on a card. Then make a duplicate set. Words of Jesus that can be used are:

> Have faith in God
> Give to the poor
> Love the Lord your God
> Make disciples of all nations
> Follow in my footsteps
> Love one another
> Be compassionate
> Proclaim the good news

Two or three children can play at one time. First they mix up the cards, then they lay them face down in four rows of four cards each. Players take turns turning over two cards to make a match. If the phrases match, the player keeps the two cards and tries again. If the two cards do not match, play passes to another player. Children continue playing until all the matches are made. This game can be played over and over again because each time it is different. This is an interesting way for children to learn the words of Jesus.

Lenten Posters. Talk with the students about positive commitments they can make during Lent. This is a good way to grow in faith and love of God. Write ideas on the board for all to see. Then assign teams of two or three to make Lenten posters with ways to grow during Lent.

Ideas for posters include:

> Share with others
> Pray each day
> Help the needy
> Be kind to all
> Forgive others
> Read the Bible
> Learn about God

Posters can be made with posterboard and colorful markers. They should feature the words of the idea plus designs, symbols, or decorations to make them attractive and interesting to read. The posters can be hung up in the hallway so that the children will be reminded to put forth extra effort during Lent. This will help students see that Lent is a time of change and growth for us as Christians.

Family Day.

Families can learn about Lent and Easter at a family day program. Families come together on a Sunday afternoon during Lent to work together on various projects relating to this season.

The program begins with prayer and song. Then families go to various activity centers of their choosing. Each center should have a person to direct the activity and help families.

It is very helpful if these center people wear butterfly nametags so people know who to ask for help. Each classroom should have a sign outside naming the activity inside. Activity centers can include:

1. Banner center. Each family adds a new life symbol to a community banner that will be hung up for Easter.

2. Seed center. Families plant seeds in paper cups to take home as a reminder of how we are to grow during Lent.

3. Mobile center. Mobiles with new life symbols are put together to be taken home.

4. Butterfly center. Each family makes a butterfly out of fabric and pipe cleaners. Magnetic tape is attached so that the butterfly can be displayed at home on the refrigerator.

5. Game center. Families play a question game together.

6. Card center. Parents and children make cards to send for Easter out of construction paper and Easter stickers.

7. Prayer center. Booklets are put together with a prayer for each day of Lent.

8. Word center. Families work together to solve a crossword puzzle about Jesus.

9. Outreach center. Placemats are made to be delivered along with dinners to homebound people.

10. Movie center. Children watch a movie with their parents.

The day concludes with punch and cookies and socializing among the families. This allows them time to share ideas and experiences with other family groups and one another.

Time of Caring

Second week of Lent prayer service

Opening: In the name of the Father, and of the Son, and of the Holy Spirit. Amen.

Greeting: This is the second week of the Lenten season. Lent is a time to remember that Jesus wants us to show love and care to all people.

Opening Song: "Reach Out" (*Hi God*)

Bible Story: This is story retold from the Bible (based on Luke 10:29-37):

Reader 1: Jesus told the people this story. One day a man was travelling down the road to Jericho. Suddenly robbers came and beat him. They took his money and left him lying by the side of the road.

Reader 2: A priest soon came by. He did not stop to help. Then a Levite came along. He saw the man, but continued on his way.

Reader 3: Finally a Samaritan man came down the road. He stopped to help the injured traveller. He bandaged the man and took him to an inn. There he paid for the man's care.

Reader 4: Jesus wants us to help other people too, like the Good Samaritan in this story. We are to have compassion for all God's people.

Reflection: Jesus used parables such as this one about the Good Samaritan to teach people. The Samaritans were a group hated by the Jewish people. It was unthinkable to them that a Samaritan would ever stop to help a Jew. They were enemies. But Jesus brought a new law of love that cuts across the barriers people make. He challenges us to live as God, our Creator, intended. He used examples from the people's everyday lives to show them and us that our relationship with God is lived out in our daily lives. We are to see all people as our neighbors.

Prayer Response: We place our petitions before the Lord.

> We pray for the poor. . .
> *Lord, hear our prayer*
> We pray for the sick. . .
> *Lord, hear our prayer*
> We pray for the lonely. . .
> *Lord, hear our prayer*
> We pray for the hungry. . .
> *Lord, hear our prayer*
> We pray for the homeless. . .
> *Lord, hear our prayer*

Song: "They'll Know We Are Christians" (*Joy Together*)

Closing Prayer: Act of Love

> O my God,
> I love you above all things
> with my whole heart and soul
> because you are all good
> and worthy of all my love.
> I love my neighbor as myself
> for love of you.
> I forgive all who have injured me
> and I ask pardon
> of all whom I have injured.

Response: In the name of the Father, and of the Son, and of the Holy Spirit. Amen.

Enrichment Ideas

Samaritan Cinquain.   Writing simple poems helps children think about the message of a bible story. A poem with a specific form is easiest for students to use. The cinquain form is as follows:

> Line 1: One word title
> Line 2: Two descriptive words
> Line 3: Three action words
> Line 4: Four descriptive words
> Line 5: One word summary

If the children are new at poetry writing, work with them on a class cinquain on the chalkboard. Then the children can work on their own individual poems. A sample of a Samaritan cinquain is:

> Samaritan
> kind person
> shared, cared, helped
> one who loved others
> neighbor

The cinquain form helps children write creatively and successfully compose a poem. Such poems help children understand the meaning of the story of the Good Samaritan.

Echo Pantomime.   To act out the story of the Good Samaritan the children can do an echo pantomime. The teacher says a line and does the motions. Then the children echo the words and actions:

Jesus told this story	(hands cup mouth)
About someone who cared:	(shake head yes)
One day a man was walking	(walk in place)
down the road to Jericho.	(point in distance)
Robbers came and hit him	(run in place)
and knocked him to the ground.	(shield face with arms)
Then the robbers ran away	(run in place)
and left the man all alone.	(close eyes, arms out)
A priest came down the road	(walk in place)
But did not stop to help.	(shake head no)

Then a Levite walked by	(walk in place)
but he did not stop to help.	(shake head no)
A Samaritan did come by	(walk in place)
and stopped to help the man.	(shake head yes)
He bandaged the man	(pretend to wrap arm)
and took him to an inn.	(walk in place)
There the man got better	(shake head yes)
and rested easily.	(hands together by head)
Jesus wants all of us	(open arms)
to help other people too.	(hold arm straight out)

This echo pantomime helps children understand the story and its message.

Time of Forgiveness

Third week of Lent prayer service

Opening: In the name of the Father, and of the Son, and of the Holy Spirit. Amen.

Greeting: This is the third week of the Lenten season. We remember that Jesus came with good news for all people. He shows us the compassion and mercy of God, our Father. God will forgive us again and again when we fail. We just have to ask. During Lent let us remember to ask for forgiveness and to resolve to live lives pleasing to God.

Opening Song: "What Shall I Do" (*Hi God 2*)

Bible Story: This is a story retold from the Bible (based on Luke 19:1-10):
 Zacchaeus had heard that Jesus was coming to his town. He was too short to see over the crowd of people who had gathered to see Jesus. But he had an idea. He climbed a tree so that he would be tall enough to see Jesus.
 Jesus came down the road. He stopped by the tree that Zacchaeus had climbed. Jesus told Zacchaeus to hurry down because they were going to his house today. So Zacchaeus came down from the tree and took Jesus to his home. There Zacchaeus told Jesus that he wouldn't cheat people anymore and that he would give half of his money to the poor.

Reflection: In this story we see how Zacchaeus responded to the coming of Jesus into his life. Jesus came with a message of forgiveness for all those who turn their lives around.
 As the story shows, it is not enough to tell God that we are sorry. We must also reconcile with the people we have hurt. Zacchaeus pledged to repay the people he had cheated and give money to the poor. We are called to change the direction of our lives toward Jesus in all things.

Prayer Response: We now ask for God's forgiveness.

For the times we have hurt others. . .
Forgive us, Father
For the times we have acted selfishly. . .
Forgive us, Father
For the times we have been slow to forgive others. . .
Forgive us, Father
For the times we have not remembered your love. . .
Forgive us, Father

Let us pause for a moment of silence to ask God's forgiveness for a time when we did not do our best. (Pause)

Song: "God Is Rich in Mercy" (*Hi God 3*)

Closing Prayer:

Dear God, loving Father of us all,
hear our prayer.
You sent Jesus to show us your forgiveness.
We ask you to forgive us for our wrongs
against you.
Forgive also our unkind words and actions.
Help us to make amends as did Zacchaeus.
May we be people who show love and mercy
to others as you show it to us.

Response: In the name of the Father, and of the Son, and of the Holy Spirit. Amen.

Enrichment Ideas

Sponge Painted Tree.   An interesting craft project for children is to make a painted tree and put Zacchaeus in it. This helps children remember the story of Zacchaeus and Jesus.

The children begin by painting a brown tree trunk and bare branches with tempera paint on sheets of white paper. Then children can decorate their trees with green leaves. Pre-mix green tempera paint with white in varying amounts to produce three different shades of green. Plastic margarine containers are good for paint and can be thrown away after use. The children use small square pieces of sponge for paint brushes and spring-type clothespins for handles. The sponges are dipped into the paint and printed onto the paper to make textured leaves. The clothespin handles keep fingers out of the paint. Children can paint a few leaves on their tree or many.

When the paint has dried, the children can add a duplicated figure of Zacchaeus. At the bottom of each picture the children should print ''Zacchaeus.'' This picture of Zacchaeus sitting in the tree will be a reminder to the children of the forgiveness Jesus brought to all people.

Discussion Questions.   Lead children in a discussion about various things we do for which we need to ask forgiveness from God and others. This helps the children think about the direction of their lives and helps them learn from one another. Questions such as the following help children think about their lives:

Is it easy to share with others?

What types of things are difficult to share?

How do you feel when someone makes an unkind remark to you?

What are some examples of remarks that hurt other people's feelings?

Do two wrongs make a right?

How often should we pray?

What are some ways to show God our love?

How can we help others as Jesus tells us to do?

Why do people get into arguments?

How does arguing make people feel?

How can you end a quarrel?

What are some ways to ask forgiveness from people?

Who are some of the people who need special kindness?

How can family members show kindness to one another?

Is it easy to tell someone that you are sorry?

This type of question helps children to talk about ways we are called to love God and others and how we sometimes fail to do this.

Bible Poster.   Children need to remember that Jesus always forgives us. No matter what we do, he will always love us. A bible poster of the Zacchaeus story can be displayed in the classroom as a reminder of Jesus' forgiveness.

Use a large sheet of posterboard. Print the words "The Story of Zacchaeus" on two lines. Then cut out bible story pictures to illustrate important moments in this story. These pictures can be found in inexpensive paperback bible story books. Direct the children as to which pictures to cut out of the book. Meaningful ones are:

> Zacchaeus at his job of tax collector
> Climbing a tree to see Jesus
> Jesus telling him to come down

Jesus at the home of Zacchaeus
Zacchaeus and his family
Giving money to the poor

Cut the pictures with rounded edges rather than squares for a more pleasing poster. Show the children how to glue them onto the posterboard. Use a glue stick so that glue does not soak through the pictures. Underneath each picture print the action shown.

This poster is a great reminder of this bible story about forgiveness. It is simple to put up and take down which is necessary if several classes use the same room. It can also be used year after year to show the story of Jesus and Zacchaeus.

Picture Story. A good way to help children remember the forgiveness that Jesus brings is a picture story. Provide picture story paper with space at the top and lines at the bottom. Encourage the children to write a summary of the story of Jesus and Zacchaeus. This will help them think about what is important in this story from the Bible and what it means.

Then ask the children to illustrate the short story that they have written with a picture in the space provided. This is an added learning experience that helps the children remember the story in yet another way. Also some children are more comfortable with drawing than writing.

The children can pick out what they felt was most important in the story to write and illustrate. This individualizes the story and helps children remember it. Hopefully, they will remember that this story shows Jesus' forgiveness for all people.

*T*ime of Prayer

Fourth week of Lent prayer service

Opening: In the name of the Father, and of the Son, and of the Holy Spirit. Amen.

Greeting: This is the fourth week of the Lenten season. During Lent and always we should strive to be a people of prayer. We need to pray to God, our Father, to praise him for all he has done in our lives and to ask his help in all things.

Opening Song: "God Is Our Father" (*Hi God*)

Bible Story: This is a story retold from the Bible (based on Matthew 6:9-15):

> Jesus told his followers to pray like this:
> Our Father, who art in heaven,
> hallowed be thy name;
> Thy kingdom come;
> thy will be done on earth
> as it is in heaven.
> Give us this day our daily bread;
> and forgive us our trespasses
> as we forgive those who trespass against us;
> and lead us not into temptation,
> but deliver us from evil.

Reflection: We are called to pray this prayer together as a community of God's people. We call God our Father for indeed he is the Father of us all. This prayer which Jesus taught us has been used throughout the centuries. It is the prayer of Christians everywhere who follow Jesus.

It is important to be people of prayer. Through prayer we ask God to help us be all that we were created to be. We ask his help to truly make his kingdom present on earth. For by ourselves we can do nothing, but with God all things become possible.

Prayer Litany: Now let us together offer a prayer of praise to God, our Father.

> For your glory. . .
> *We praise you, God*
> For making us your children. . .
> *We praise you, God*
> For loving each of us. . .
> *We praise you, God*
> For sending Jesus to teach us. . .
> *We praise you, God*

Song: "Lord, Hear Our Prayer" (*Living God's Word*)

Closing Prayer: Now let us pray together the prayer Jesus taught us. (say the Our Father)

Response: In the name of the Father, and of the Son, and of the Holy Spirit. Amen.

Enrichment Ideas

Prayer Display.   A simple idea that can help children remember to pray the Our Father is a display of this prayer. Before class time type out the words to the Our Father and duplicate enough copies for each child.

Each of the children needs to find a nature picture that illustrates this prayer. Travel booklets are terrific for this project because they contain lovely mountain and river scenes. Such booklets are available free of charge by writing to state tourist bureaus. Encourage the children to pick a picture that they like. Then ask them to trim their pictures to the same size as the prayer.

Give each child a half sheet of construction paper. Provide colors that coordinate with the pictures that they have selected. Instruct the children to fold their paper in half and round off the top corners with a scissors. Then they can glue the picture on the left side and the prayer on the right side.

This prayer display can be used at home as a reminder to say this prayer that Jesus taught. It can be displayed as both a call to prayer and a reminder of God's presence in our lives.

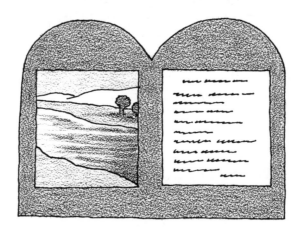

Praise the Lord Mural.   We praise God through our words and our actions. It is important that children learn that they are to show praise to God in their lives. A Praise the Lord mural can help them express praise to God, our Father and Creator. It also helps them remember the importance of praising God in many different ways.

This idea can be used by children of all ages. The only ingredients are paint, paper and imagination. The background for the mural is a long sheet of butcher paper. In the middle of the paper paint the words "Praise the Lord" in large letters.

Provide a variety of colors of tempera paint with which the children can decorate the mural. Use some unusual colors also such as purple to give it a distinctive look. White paint mixed in with the other colors gives different shades of color. Powdered tempera is easy to mix and very economical.

Ask each child to paint a decoration on the mural using a large paint brush. It can be a curvy line, zig zag. a swirl, or any decoration the child chooses to make. Encourage creativity in the type of design and the color choice. When the mural is dry, display it in the classroom or wherever the children pray to remind them to always praise the Lord.

Prayer Book.   A book about prayer is a good way to help young children learn. An excellent book is *I Can Talk to God . . . Anytime, Anyplace* by Jennie Davis (see the Directory). Through simple words and colorful pictures, this book shows how young children can make prayer a part of their daily lives. When they are with family, friends, or alone they can talk to God. Anywhere they are, God will listen to them. This book can also be used to lead into a discussion with the children of the many ways that we can pray in our lives. Prayer should be woven into the fabric of our everyday existence. It should be an important part of who we are as Christians.

Time of Faith

Fifth week of Lent prayer service

Opening: In the name of the Father, and of the Son, and of the Holy Spirit. Amen.

Greeting: This is the fifth week of the Lenten season. Lent is a good time to remember that as Christians we are people of faith in Jesus Christ who must live what we believe.

Opening Song: "I Want to Walk in the Presence of God" (*Hi God 2*)

Bible Story: This is a story retold from the Bible (based on Mark 10:46-52):
    In the crowd at Jericho was a blind man named Bartimaeus. When he heard that Jesus was coming, he called out to him. He asked Jesus to have pity on him. People told him to be quiet, but Bartimaeus shouted again to Jesus to have pity.
    Jesus stopped and asked Bartimaeus what he wanted. The blind man said that he wanted to see. Jesus told Bartimaeus to go on his way. He had been healed because of his great faith. Now Bartimaeus could see. Immediately he began to follow Jesus.

Reflection: This is a story about faith. The blind man believed in Jesus. He could see Jesus in his heart. He had faith. Jesus cured his blindness and Bartimaeus became a follower of Jesus.
    This story is a reminder to all of us that we are called to be people of faith in Jesus. Jesus came to show us the way to the Father. We must not be blind to what is really important in life. Instead we must listen to Jesus in our hearts and live as his followers. We must have faith.

Prayer Litany: Now we ask the Lord to listen to our petitions.

> Help us to follow your way. . .
>   *Lord, hear our prayer*
> Be with us in all that we do. . .
>   *Lord, hear our prayer*

Guide us to live as you showed us. . .
Lord, hear our prayer
Enrich our faith in you. . .
Lord, hear our prayer
Fill us with your love. . .
Lord, hear our prayer
Enable us to proclaim the good news. . .
Lord, hear our prayer

Song: "Jesus You Have the Power to Heal" (*Hi God 2*)

Closing Prayer: Let us pray together the Act of Faith.

O my God, I firmly believe
that you are one God in three divine Persons,
Father, Son, and Holy Spirit.
I believe that your divine Son became man
and died for our sins,
and will come to judge the living and the dead.
I believe in all that you have revealed
because you can neither deceive
nor be deceived.

Response: In the name of the Father, and of the Son, and of the Holy Spirit. Amen.

Enrichment Ideas

Felt Symbol Banner.   As Christians we believe in Jesus as did the blind man. A banner with symbols can help remind children what we believe. Symbols of a cross to represent Jesus, a fish to represent Christians, and a heart to symbolize love can be placed on individual felt banners as a message without words.

Each child needs a 9″ wide by 13″ long piece of felt to make a banner. The top inch is folded down and glued along the edge to form a pocket. The bottom can be cut into points for a decorative effect. Blue felt provides a good background color and is sold by the yard in fabric stores.

The symbols should be explained to the children. Provide green felt out of which each child can cut a cross. A fish can be cut out of gold felt. Red is an appropriate color for a heart. Provide patterns for these symbols. When the children have each cut out their symbols, they can glue them onto their individual banners.

In order to display the banners, give each child a 10″ long wooden dowel to put through the top. These are sold in variety stores, craft stores and home centers. Provide green yarn so that the children can tie a piece to both ends of the dowel to form a hanger. Names on masking tape on the back of the banners will help prevent mixups when the children take home their banners. These banners are a reminder that Christians have faith in Jesus and know his love.

Echo Pantomime. Activities such as echo pantomimes are an important aid to working with children. Echo pantomiming a bible story helps children understand it. The teacher says the words and does the actions. The children echo the words and actions line by line.

Jesus led his disciples	(beckon with arm)
to the town of Jericho.	(walk in place)
A man named Bartimaeus was there	(nod head)
who was blind and could not see.	(hand over eyes)
When Bartimaeus heard Jesus	(hand behind ear)
he was very happy.	(nod head)
Bartimaeus called out,	(hands cup mouth)
"Jesus have pity on me."	(fold hands)
People said to him,	(point in distance)
"Be quiet, Bartimaeus."	(finger over mouth)
But Bartimaeus called again	(hands cup mouth)
"Jesus have pity on me."	(fold hands)
Jesus stopped walking	(walk in place, stop)
and told Bartimaeus to come near.	(beckon with arm)
Jesus said to him,	(hands cup mouth)
"What do you want from me?"	(point to self)
"I want to see," he said.	(point to eyes)
Jesus said, "Your faith is great"	(nod head)
and Bartimaeus was healed.	(hand over eyes, remove)
He began to follow Jesus	(walk in place)
for he believed with all his heart.	(hand over heart)

Doing the actions in an echo pantomime helps children understand the words.

Good News Telegram.   This activity helps children put the story of Jesus and the blind man into their own words. This aids understanding and retention. Ask each child to write a telegram about the good news Jesus brings in this bible story.

Explain to the children that a telegram is a short way of sending a message. Make telegram forms for them to use. On half sheets of yellow paper put Good News Telegram at the top in large letters. Instruct the children that instead of using periods, they should use the word "stop" to indicate the end of a sentence. Thus a good news telegram about the blind man turns out like this:

Today Jesus cured blind man   Stop   All are amazed at miracle   Stop   Blind man now follows Jesus   Stop   Details to follow   Stop

This is an interesting way for children to compose a summary of this bible story. They have to think about what is important in order to put it into words on their telegram.

Time of Giving

Opening: In the name of the Father, and of the Son, and of the Holy Spirit. Amen.

Greeting: This is a very special week in the church year called Holy Week. Holy Week includes Palm Sunday, Holy Thursday, Good Friday and Holy Saturday. It is the week just before Easter.

During this time we commemorate the events of the last week of Jesus' life. God so loved his people that he sent his only Son to us. Through all that Jesus said and did, he redeemed us. He came for all of us. He led us back to the Father to share in his divine life.

Opening Song: "His Banner Over Me Is Love" (*Hi God*)

Bible Reading: This is a reading from the gospel of Matthew (26:26-28):

"While they were eating, Jesus took bread, said the blessing, broke it, and giving it to his disciples said, 'Take and eat; this is my body.' Then he took a cup, gave thanks, and gave it to them, saying, 'Drink from it, all of you, for this is my blood.'"

Reflection: This reading tells the story of the Last Supper. The Eucharist today is to be the center of our lives as Christians. In the Eucharist we encounter Jesus Christ himself. Through sharing his body and blood in this sacrament, Jesus is with us so that we are strengthened and renewed.

Through his Last Supper, cross, and resurrection Jesus gave himself to his Father and to all people. He continues to redeem us and be with us through his gift of the Eucharist. Our community celebration unites us to God and to one another. Through the Eucharist we offer God the perfect gift, his Son.

Prayer Litany: Now let us pray.

>May we be people who care. . .
>>*Hear us, Lord*
>
>May we be people who forgive. . .
>>*Hear us, Lord*
>
>May we be people who share. . .
>>*Hear us, Lord*
>
>May we be people who pray. . .
>>*Hear us, Lord*
>
>May we be people who love. . .
>>*Hear us, Lord*

Song: "A Sign of His Love" (*Jesus Is With Us*)

Closing Prayer:

>Dear God,
>During this Holy Week hear our prayers that
>   we may always remember your great love.
>You sent your Son to redeem us so that we
>   could be recreated in him.
>Help us to remember that you are with us,
>   now and forever.

Response: In the name of the Father, and of the Son, and of the Holy Spirit. Amen.

Enrichment Ideas

Holy Week Booklet.   To help children understand the events of Holy Week, help them make a booklet. Use half sheets of paper for each page. The cover page will proclaim "Holy Week." The inside pages are Palm Sunday, Holy Thursday and Good Friday. At the end include an Easter page to show that all the events of Holy Week culminated in Jesus' resurrection.

On each page have children color or draw an appropriate symbol for each special day. Next to each picture they can print an explanation of the day or an appropriate bible quote.

Let the children staple the pages together for their own individual Holy Week booklet. This activity helps children bring together and understand some of the important events of this final week of Jesus' life. This week is central to our beliefs as Christians. Each child will have a Holy Week booklet to take home as a reminder of God's love for us.

Seder Meal.   A terrific way for children to experience Holy Week is through a seder meal.[10] The children learn about the Jewish feast of Passover which Jesus celebrated with his friends.

Tables are set up with the appropriate foods and dishes. Children are seated. An adult acts as the leader.

The meal begins with the traditional lighting of the candles. Then the leader holds up each item of food and explains its meaning:

The seder cup. The seder cup is the cup of wine set aside for Elijah,the prophet. The Jewish people believe that he will one day return to bring peace to this world. The seder cup is set on the table, and the door is left open to welcome him.

The kiddush. (wine) Blessed are you, O Lord, God of creation, King of the universe, who created this sweetness of wine, symbol of joy and gladness, we thank you for this beauty of home and love of family. (All drink a sip of wine.)

The egg. (hard-boiled) This egg symbolizes the festival offering Jewish pilgrims presented to God at the Temple in Jerusalem. At the seder this egg becomes a sign of mourning for the destruction of the Temple.

The korpas. (bitter herbs) This parsley dipped in salt water symbolizes the meager diet of the Jewish people while they were slaves in Egypt. The salt water into which the parsley is dipped represents the salt tears the Jewish slaves cried.

The mah-geed. We will now listen carefully to the mah-geed. These are traditional questions asked by a child at every passover meal. (In place of the traditional answers, include the scripture readings from the Mass of the Lord's Supper. Four children ask the questions and four other children do the readings.)

Question: Why is this night different from all other nights?
   Reading: Exodus 12:1-8
Question: Why do all of us eat this bread together tonight?
   Reading: 1 Corinthians 11:23-24
Question: Why do all of us drink wine together tonight?
   Reading: 1 Corinthians 11:25-26
Question: Why should all of us be here together tonight?
   Reading: John 13:1-5
Leader: Let us praise God!
   All: Psalm 148

The pesah. (lamb shankbone) This shankbone represents the pesah lamb sacrificed in the temple.

The matzos. (unleavened bread) Blessed are you, O Lord, King of the universe, who brings forth bread from the earth. When the Jews were in the desert they ate manna; when the Jews were in Palestine, they ate bread. But the night they left Egypt they had no time to wait for the bread to rise, so they ate unleavened bread.
   We, too, are on a journey, a journey of faith, of celebration, of preparation for the Kingdom of God. (The matzos are broken into pieces and distributed to the children to eat.) Jesus is with us! Through this eating we show that we want to be united with each other in Jesus. Bless this food, Jesus, which we eat as a sign of our union with you.

The moror. (radishes) The radishes, or moror, are served as a reminder of the bitter days of slavery in Egypt. (Radishes are distributed.) Blessed are you, O Lord God, who has sanctified us by your commandments. Thank you for letting us taste the bitterness of slavery so we may appreciate more your gift of freedom.

The haroset. (mixture of chopped apples, honey, and wine) This represents the cement the Jews used in laying bricks during their time of slavery. It is sweet because it represents the kindness of God, who makes even slavery bearable. (Some haroset on a piece of matzo is distributed to each person.)

Leader: Let us pray. May God give us strength.

All: Amen.

Leader: May God bless all who are assembled at our seder table.

All: Amen.

Leader: May God send blessings to our houses, families and those near and dear to us.

All: Amen.

Leader: May he who grants peace in heaven grant peace and freedom to all persons.

All: Amen.

Way of the Cross

Good Friday prayer service

Opening: In the name of the Father, and of the Son, and of the Holy Spirit. Amen.

Greeting: We come here to remember the experiences of Jesus on Good Friday, the day he died on the cross. We commemorate his suffering and death out of love for us. We remember also his resurrection from the dead three days later. Today we walk the way of the cross with Jesus.

STATIONS OF THE CROSS

First station: *Jesus Is Condemned to Die.*

Jesus is told that he will be put to death although he has done nothing wrong. Jesus came to call us all to God, but the people rejected him. Pilate orders Jesus to be crucified.

Prayer: Dear Jesus, help us recognize your truth in our lives. May we never turn away from you and your love. Help us to do what you ask of us.

Second station: *Jesus Takes Up His Cross.*

Jesus died so that all of us could live. He walks toward Calvary treated like a common criminal. He carries the burden of our sins out of love.

Prayer: Dear Jesus, help us carry our small crosses. May we not become discouraged, but remember that you are with us.

Third station: *Jesus Falls the First Time.*

Jesus, weakened by scourging, falls under the weight of the cross. He does not give up, but rises to meet his destiny. He came into the world to lead us back to God and he will finish what he set out to do.

Prayer: Dear Jesus, help us be like you. Help us to try again and again even when it is not easy.

Fourth station: *Jesus Meets His Mother.*

Jesus, carrying his cross, sees his mother. Her heart breaks with sadness that her Son must suffer so.

Prayer: Dear Jesus, help us be there for one another in time of sadness and suffering. Help us not turn away from someone who needs us.

Fifth station: *Simon Helps Jesus Carry His Cross.*

Simon of Cyrene is told to carry the cross behind Jesus. The Roman soldiers did not want Jesus to die on the way.

Prayer: Dear Jesus, you suffered so much out of love. Strengthen us to help those who suffer greatly in our world. May we see your face in them.

Sixth station: *Veronica Wipes the Face of Jesus.*

A woman named Veronica came up to Jesus and wiped his face out of compassion. She steps out from the crowd, not caring what people will think.

Prayer: Dear Jesus, help us to not depend upon what other people think of us. Never let that stop us from what we have to do. Help us put you first in our lives.

Seventh station: *Jesus Falls the Second Time.*

Jesus is weak and falls again. Bruised and shaken, he manages to stand up and continue his journey to the cross.

Prayer: Dear Jesus, you came to earth as a man to show us the way to God. Help us remember we can always turn to you with our problems and you will understand.

Eighth station: *Jesus Meets the Women.*

Friends of Jesus were in the crowd along the way to the cross. They were sad to see what was being done to him. Jesus turned and spoke to them. He cared about people despite his own pain.

Prayer: Dear Jesus, help us to have compassion for others. May we work for the good of all people in our world. Help us look beyond our own problems to see the needs of others.

Ninth station: *Jesus Falls a Third Time.*

Jesus, tired and in pain, falls yet another time. He carries the rejection of those he came to save. He summons up the strength to go on to his death.

Prayer: Dear Jesus, help us continue on even when we become discouraged. Help us center our lives on you as we journey in faith to the Father.

Tenth station: *Jesus Is Stripped of His Clothing.*

The Roman soldiers took Jesus clothing. They treated him without respect and tried to take away his dignity.

Prayer: Dear Jesus, help us remember that it is not our possessions that are important, but what we do to make God's kingdom a reality in our world. Help us treat others with respect and compassion in your name.

Eleventh station: *Jesus Is Crucified.*

Jesus is nailed to the cross and lifted up between heaven and earth. Out of love he suffers on our behalf for our sins and our failings.

Prayer: Dear Jesus, help us to remember your great love for us. You accepted what was to come. Be with us always.

Twelfth station: *Jesus Dies on the Cross.*

Jesus is executed as a common criminal on his cross at Calvary. He gave us everything he had, even his life.

Prayer: Dear Jesus, you gave up your life for us. May we live our lives for you. Help us follow your way in all things.

Thirteenth station: *Jesus Is Taken Down from the Cross.*

Joseph of Arimathea had been a secret disciple. He now comes forward to ask Pilate for permission to take down the body of Jesus.

Prayer: Dear Jesus, help us have the courage to follow you publicly in all things. May we come forward when it matters and not be afraid.

Fourteenth station: *Jesus Is Laid in the Tomb.*

The body of Jesus is wrapped in a linen cloth and placed in a new tomb. A large rock is moved over the entrance to seal it. But three days later Jesus rises from the dead. By his life, death and resurrection he redeems the world.

Prayer: Dear Jesus, we are sorry for all our sins. Help us always remember your great love. We ask for forgiveness when we fail and know that you will always grant it. We praise you for the new life you bring to all people.

Song: "Behold the Wood" (*A Dwelling Place*)

Closing Prayer: Dear God, out of love for us you sent your only Son, Jesus. Help us to say yes to your call in our lives. We acknowledge our failings and weaknesses and ask your help to live lives pleasing to you. May we follow the example of Jesus Christ in all we do. Help us remember your great love for us not only today, but always.

Response: In the name of the Father, and of the Son, and of the Holy Spirit. Amen.

Enrichment Ideas

Hot Cross Buns.   Hot cross buns are traditional for Lent and Good Friday. These pastries are made with a white icing cross on the top of each one as a reminder of Jesus. Hot cross buns can be homemade or are available ready to eat at grocery stores and bakeries. They can be served to the children as a commemoration of Christ's cross and the idea that we call this day good because of God's love for us. The story of Good Friday is not complete until Easter. The cross leads to the resurrection and so we celebrate what Jesus has done.

Painted Paperweight.   Children can make a Good Friday paperweight with rocks and markers. Students can bring rocks from their yards at home. Ask some children to bring extras.

On each rock the children use a marker to draw a cross and print the word "Jesus" next to it. These painted rocks can be used as paperweights at home. They are a reminder of Jesus' death on the cross for us. Through his death we will have new life with him.

Cross Collage.   A craft activity featuring a cross can be made from construction paper.[11] The children need sheets of black construction paper 9″ high by 8″ wide for the background for their cross collage. Each child cuts out a piece of green paper to look like a stained glass window. This is glued onto the background sheet. The children then cut out a brown cross 7″ high by 5″ wide and glue it in the center of the green window.

Next give the children pieces of construction paper in a variety of colors such as purple, orange, yellow and red. Each child needs to cut out about 14 small triangles. This is easily accomplished by cutting out squares and then cutting them in half diagonally. The children glue the triangles onto the green paper in the space at the sides of the cross.

This produces a cross collage for Good Friday. It looks like a stained glass window. This project helps show children the meaning of Good Friday. It hints at the new life to come with the green color and the bursts of other colors visible behind the cross. Something great was to happen as a result of Jesus' public death on the cross.

Jesus Is Risen

Easter prayer service

Opening: In the name of the Father, and of the Son, and of the Holy Spirit. Amen.

Greeting: We will soon celebrate the great feast of Easter. Because of the resurrection of Jesus Christ, we all have new life with God. Easter brought the dawn of a new age to all people through Jesus.

Song: "New Hope" (*Hi God 2*)

Bible Story: This is the story of Easter retold from the Bible (based on Mark 16:1-7):

Narrator: Just after sunrise on Sunday morning, the women went to the tomb of Jesus to anoint him with oils. This was their burial custom. On the way there they asked one another,

Voice 1: "Who will move the big stone away from the entrance to the tomb so that we can go inside?"

Narrator: When they arrived at the tomb, they found that the huge stone had already been rolled back. They entered the tomb and were frightened when they saw a young man in a white robe there. The angel spoke to them,

Voice 2: "Do not be afraid. You are looking for Jesus. He has been raised up. He is not here. You will see him soon as he promised.

Narrator: After listening to the angel, the women quickly left the tomb. Later, Jesus appeared to his followers.

Reflection: Through this bible story we witness the events of the first Easter morning when Jesus rose from the dead to a new life. The resurrection of Jesus is at the heart of our Christian faith. Jesus has conquered death for all of us. Through him we become sharers in God's divine life. We are also to be transformed by Easter. We are to live our lives with hope. We are to be witnesses in the world to all that Jesus said and did.

Prayer Response: Now let us pray together.

Jesus is risen. . .
Alleluia. Alleluia.
He brings us new life. . .
Alleluia. Alleluia.
He is always with us. . .
Alleluia. Alleluia.
He shows us the Father's love. . .
Alleluia. Alleluia.
We are an Easter people. . .
Alleluia. Alleluia.

Closing Song: "O Yes, Lord Jesus Lives" (*Hi God 2*).

Closing Prayer:

God our loving Father
　　we are your people
and everything in us shouts out for joy
　　on this feast of the Resurrection.

What great love and power
　　you have shown!
You have raised your Son Jesus
　　from death!
You have given him a new life
　　stronger than death.
You have made him Lord
　　over all the earth.

In the name of all your creatures
We thank you for your great love.
We praise you
　　and we wait with hope
　　for the day
　　of our own resurrection.

Show us that we can celebrate
　　the new life of Easter
　　today and every day
　　through the truth,
　　the hope,
　　and the love
　　we give each other
　　in the name of our risen Lord.[12]

Response: In the name of the Father, and of the Son, and of the
Holy Spirit. Amen.

Enrichment Ideas

Hope Banner.   Each child can make a banner to proclaim the hope Jesus brought to us at Easter. Beige burlap makes a neutral banner background and is sold by the yard in fabric stores. Each child needs a precut piece 15″ long by 10″ wide. Enlist parent help to cut out the burlap pieces. Also ask a parent to fold over the top inch of each banner and sew a line of stitching across it to form a rod pocket.

Use bright spring colors of fabric such as blue and green with a small print design such as flowers. From the blue fabric the children cut out a butterfly and a flower as new life symbols. Out of the green fabric the children cut letters spelling "Hope" plus a center for the flower and a body for the butterfly.

The children glue the letters onto the banner going diagonally down the middle. Then they glue the butterfly in the upper right corner and the flower in the lower left corner. Next the center is glued on top of the flower and the body on top of the butterfly for contrast.

The edges of the banner can be fringed slightly by pulling the two outside threads. A wooden dowel is then slipped through the top pocket of each banner. An 18″ length of green yarn tied to either end of the dowel makes a hanger. The hope banner helps children remember what Easter means to them as Christians and can be displayed at home for Easter.

Easter Egg Hunt. A traditional way for younger children to celebrate Easter is with an egg hunt. Older children can help organize this event and supervise the younger children.

Begin the activities with games for the children to play. Interesting games include the following:

Egg and spoon race. Each child is given a plastic egg to balance on a spoon. At a given signal all the children race for the finish line. If the egg falls out of the spoon during the race, the child must stop and replace it before continuing the race.

Basket relay. The children line up in teams. The first person on each team is handed an Easter basket. When the signal is given, the children run over and pick up a plastic egg from the pile and place it in their basket. Then they run back to the next child in line and pass on the basket. This continues until one teams finishes first.

Hopping race. All the children line up. When they hear the word "go" they hop on both feet like bunnies across the grass until they reach the finish line.

Bunny relay. The children are divided into teams. Children in each team line up one behind the other. The first child in each line is handed a stuffed bunny. When the signal is given, the children with the bunnies race up to the finish line and back again. Then they hand the bunny on to the next child in line on their team. That child runs up and back and so on until all the children on one team have completed the relay.

The children can be awarded candy prizes for first, second and third place in each event. Also ribbons can be given to all those who participate. These can be made from construction paper with an Easter sticker at the top.

The events conclude with the Easter egg hunt. The children are grouped by age so that bigger and faster children do not have the advantage. Wrapped, candy eggs are hidden in the grass in a separate area. When they hear "go" the children hunt for the eggs and get to keep any that they find. Each child should bring a basket for the egg hunt in which they can put the eggs. These activities are a fun way for younger children to share in the Easter activties and excitement.

Blooming Tulips. All around us at Easter we see signs of new life. A good project for younger children is a paper pot of tulips. This is a reminder of the new life of spring and the new life Jesus brings to us.

Each child needs a blue background sheet to represent the sky. The children need access to wallpaper sample books out of which they can cut brightly colored tulips. Because each wallpaper sample is different, each child's tulips will be unique. Then show the children how to cut out green paper stems and leaves for their tulips. A pot for the flowers can be cut out of construction paper to coordinate with the colors of the tulips.

The children glue their paper pot onto the background sheet. Then they make their flowers grow by gluing on the stems and leaves and flowers. A piece of green ric rac can be glued to the rim of the pot for decoration and a final touch. The bright tulips look like they are blooming in the springtime. At the bottom of the page be sure each child prints "Easter brings new life" as a reminder. This project is interesting for the children and helps them remember the new life of Easter. Spring is a miracle we witness anew each year.

Easter brings new life

Coming of the Holy Spirit

Pentecost prayer service

Opening: In the name of the Father who created us, the Son who redeemed us, and the Holy Spirit who lives in us. Amen.

Greeting: This Sunday we will celebrate the great feast of Pentecost. We remember how Jesus sent the Holy Spirit to be with his apostles. That same Holy Spirit lives in each one of us today.

Opening Song: "Lord, Send Out Your Spirit" (*Jesus and His Friends*)

Bible Reading: This is the story of Pentecost from the Acts of the Apostles (2:1-4).
  "When the time for Pentecost was fulfilled they were all in one place together. And suddenly there came from the sky a noise like a strong driving wind and it filled the entire house in which they were. Then there appeared to them tongues as of fire which parted and came to rest on each one of them. And they were all filled with the holy Spirit."

Reflection: In this reading we see the promise of Jesus to his followers fulfilled. He sent the Holy Spirt to them to be present in their lives and in their work.
  The feast of Pentecost is the birthday of the church. The very word *church* means assembly. We are an assembly of God's people united in Christ through the Holy Spirit. The church is to make Christ visible in the world so that people will come to know his love.
  As followers of Jesus Christ we are to proclaim the good news of his life, death and resurrection. We are to come together as a community of God's people to give praise to God for his Son, Jesus. We are to make the teachings of Jesus Christ a reality in our lives and in the world. We are to work together for the good of all people. The Holy Spirit lives in the heart of each one of us to guide us on this journey. Created by the Father we are to follow the Son with the help of the Holy Spirit in our lives.

Prayer Response: Let us together ask the help of the Holy Spirit in our lives.

> Strengthen us in faith . . .
> > *Come, Holy Spirit*
> Fill us with love . . .
> > *Come, Holy Spirit*
> Enable us to hope . . .
> > *Come, Holy Spirit*
> Direct our lives . . .
> > *Come, Holy Spirit*
> Help us to follow Jesus . . .
> > *Come, Holy Spirit*

Closing Song: "The Spirit Is a-Movin'" (*Hi God*)

Closing Prayer:

> Glory be to the Father,
> > and to the Son,
> > and to the Holy Spirit.
> As it was in the beginning,
> > is now,
> > and will be forever.

Response: In the name of the Father, and of the Son, and of the Holy Spirit. Amen.

Enrichment Ideas

Symbol Window. Stained glass windows have been an art form used for hundreds of years to remind us of what we believe as Christians. Children can make paper windows with symbols of our beliefs as a craft project.

Each child should cut out a church window shape with a rounded top from black paper. Then have them cut out four different colored paper squares and glue them onto the window like panes of colored glass. Be sure that some black shows between the squares like the lead in stained glass.

The next step is for the children to cut out four symbols using contrasting colors of paper. Christian symbols that can be used include a fish (Christian), cross (Jesus), shell (baptism), candle (light of world), chalice and host (Eucharist), triangle (trinity), and butterfly (resurrection). The four symbols are then glued onto the four colored squares. For example, a yellow cross can be glued onto a blue square or an orange fish onto a green square. This makes a bright paper window with symbols of beliefs held in common by members of the church Jesus founded. The symbols represent our belief in Jesus and our willingness to follow the Holy Spirit in our lives.

Christian Diamente. Children learn a great deal from creating poems about what it means to be a Christian. In order to write a poem, they have to reflect on what it is to be a follower of Jesus Christ. The diamente poetry form is a poem written in a diamond shape.

> 1st line = 1 word (noun)
> 2nd line = 2 words (verb and noun)
> 3rd line = 3 words ("ing" words)
> 4th line = 4 words (phrase)
> 5th line = 3 words ("ing" words)
> 6th line = 2 words (verb and noun)
> 7th line = 1 word (noun)

A Christian diamente turns out like this:

Christians

follow Jesus

helping   praying   loving

tell   the   good   news

caring   hoping   sharing

love   others

us

The class can work together on a diamente. Go line by line with them through the form. Write the children's ideas on the board until the poem is finished. Then the children can try to compose their own poems about being a Christian.

Person of Faith

May procession prayer service

Opening: In the name of the Father, and of the Son, and of the Holy Spirit. Amen.

Greeting: During the month of May we traditionally honor Mary as the mother of God. We are gathered here today to hear her story and learn by her example.

Opening Song: "Gentle Woman" (*Celebrating God's Life*)

Bible Story: This is a story retold from the Bible (based on Luke 1:26-38):

There was a girl named Mary who lived in the town of Nazareth. God sent the angel, Gabriel, as a messenger to her. Mary was afraid, but the angel told her that she had found favor with God. She was to become the mother of his Son, Jesus. Mary said yes to God. She would serve him with her life.

Reflection: In this story we see how Mary said yes to God. She is a model to all of us as Christians. We too need to say yes with our lives to what God asks of us. Mary was a person of great faith who lived that faith in all she did. We honor her today as the Mother of God and of all of us.

May Procession: Now please come forward to honor Mary by bringing flowers to place in front of her statue. (Direct the children to come two by two and place their flowers in baskets while "Hail Mary" (*Hi God 2*) plays in the background.)

Prayer Response: Now let us pray together.

> Mary, mother of God . . .
>> *Pray for us*
> Mary, caring and loving person . . .
>> *Pray for us*

Mary, person of great faith . . .
Pray for us
Mary, mother of us all . . .
Pray for us

Closing Song: "Immaculate Mary" (traditional)

Closing Prayer: We now pray the prayer to Mary:

Hail Mary, full of grace,
the Lord is with you.
Blessed are you among women
and blessed is the fruit of your womb, Jesus.
Holy Mary, mother of God,
pray for us sinners,
now and at the hour of our death.

Response: In the name of the Father, and of the Son, and of the Holy Spirit. Amen.

Enrichment Ideas

Prayer Chain.   The Hail Mary is a prayer to be memorized so that we can pray it together in times of joy and in times of sorrow. To help children learn this prayer, show them how to make a colorful prayer chain.[13]

Provide eight strips of paper for each child. Each strip should be a different color. Strips can be cut most easily and quickly with a paper cutter. Also make a large copy of the Hail Mary that the children can use for reference.

On each strip the children print a phrase from this prayer. The eighth strip is for the Amen. Allow the children to consult with and help one another with this project. Strips can be preprinted and duplicated for younger children.

When the children have finished printing their strips, they assemble the chain by looping the strips together with tape. The links must be assembled in the correct order of saying the Hail Mary. This is an interesting way for children to reinforce their knowledge of this important traditional prayer.

Rosary.   The rosary has been a popular devotion since the 15th century. It is thought to have been begun by St. Dominic who received it from Our Lady. Explain the rosary to the children as a circle of prayers to Mary. Show them how the beads count the prayers that are said.

An important part of saying the rosary is thinking about the various mysteries. Each decade is a different mystery. Explain the mysteries of the rosary to the children so that they can become familiar with them. The 15 mysteries of the rosary are:

The Joyful Mysteries

Annunciation to Mary
Visit of Mary to Elizabeth
Birth of Jesus
Presentation of Jesus
Finding Jesus in the temple

The Sorrowful Mysteries

Agony in the Garden
Scourging of Jesus
Crowning with thorns
Carrying the cross
Crucifixion of Jesus

The Glorious Mysteries

Resurrection of Jesus
Ascension of Jesus
Coming of the Holy Spirit
Assumption of Mary into heaven
Crowning of Mary as Queen of heaven

These events of the lives of Jesus and his mother, Mary, are mysteries of our faith. When the rosary is said, the mystery is named at the beginning of each decade and kept in mind while the prayers are said. Thus the rosary is a means not only of prayer, but of meditation.

Action Rhyme.   Action rhymes help children understand and learn by being involved. This action rhyme about Mary helps the children understand the story of Mary and why she is so special. It is especially good for younger children.[14]

An angel came to Mary,	(hands form halo)
and said, God has chosen you	(point)
to have a special baby	(cradle arms)
because your love is true.	(hands on heart)
You will call him Jesus	(shake head)
and everyone will know	(open arms wide)
he's a special gift from God	(nod)
because he loves us so.	(hug self)

This action rhyme makes the example of Mary more memorable to the children because they actively learn by doing. Like all of us, they remember more of what they do than what is just told to them.

Mother's Day.   It is appropriate that Mother's Day comes during the month when we honor Mary. Young children can learn about Mary by thinking of the various things that she probably did for Jesus as he was growing up. She most likely taught him, cooked his meals, took him places, made his clothes, and other things that needed to be done. This helps children see Mary as a real person who did her best for her Son and who lived a life of caring and love.

Encourage the children to make Mother's Day cards for their mother, grandmother, aunt, or other special person who shows love to them as Mary showed love to Jesus. Cards can be made from construction paper and markers. Be sure the children sign their names on the inside of the cards they make. Remind the children God wants us to show care and love to others as Mary did.

*P*eople of Peace

End-of-year prayer service

Opening: In the name of the Father, and of the Son, and of the Holy Spirit. Amen.

Greeting: As we end this school year, let us go forth as followers of Jesus to live in peace with others.

Opening Song: "Peace To You and Me" (*Hi God 3*)

Bible Story: This is a reading from the letter of Paul to the Colossians (3:12-15):
    "Put on then, as God's chosen ones, holy and beloved, heartfelt compassion, kindness, humility, gentleness, and patience, bearing with one another and forgiving one another, if one has a grievance against another; as the Lord has forgiven you, so must you also do. And over all these put on love, that is, the bond of perfection. And let the peace of Christ control your hearts, the peace into which you were also called in one body."

Reflection: In this reading Paul reminds us that we are to be caring and forgiving people who live in peace. Jesus treated other people with kindness and compassion and so must we. As people who call ourselves Christian, we must be concerned about the needs and suffering of others. We must respect the dignity of each human being and strive to be peacemakers in the world. We must be a people of peace because we care about others in Jesus' name.

Sign of Peace: As a sign that we will try to be people of peace, let us turn to one another and offer them a sign of peace in the name of Jesus. (Children shake hands and extend the greeting "peace be with you" to one another.)

Prayer Litany: Now let us together offer our petitions to God.

> Where there is suffering . . .
> *May there be peace*

Where there is injustice . . .
May there be peace
Where there is hatred . . .
May there be peace
Where there is discrimination . . .
May there be peace
Where there is war . . .
May there be peace

Closing Song: "Peace Time" (*Hi God*)

Closing Prayer:

Dear God,
We go forth strengthened in faith
by your love.
Help us to be a people of peace
to others.
May we proclaim the good news that
Jesus brought to one and all.
Be with us in all that we do
now and forever.

Response: In the name of the Father, and of the Son, and of the Holy Spirit. Amen.

Enrichment Ideas

Words of Peace.   We begin to make peace a reality in a small way by the actions and words in our own lives. Peace starts with the way we treat one another each day. Talk with the children and remind them that peace is everyone's responsibility. We are to look beyond people's differences to see that all people are created by God and loved by him. As Christians we are to be a people of peace.

All of us need to work hard at resolving conflicts when they arise. Small conflicts can lead to big conflicts. Ask the children to think about ways they can make peace in their own lives. We need to learn to say "I'm sorry" and "please forgive me." All of us need to look beyond our own selfish concerns and see the hurt and needs of others.

Not only must we learn to ask forgiveness, but we must learn to grant it to others in our lives. Ask the children to think about times when it has been difficult to forgive someone who has hurt them. Remind them that in the Our Father we ask God to forgive us as we forgive others. We must be a people of forgiveness who care about others. We must share God's love and caring with other people. We must be a people of peace in our lives who also help others find peace in theirs.

Peace Wreath.   A class project to which all the children can contribute is a peace wreath.[15] This can be made for display on the class bulletin board as a reminder that as followers of Jesus we must strive for peace in our lives and in the world.

Cut a large 14″ circle from posterboard. Then cut away a large circle from the middle to form a 2″ wide rim. Provide red paper out of which the children can each cut a 4″ red heart for the wreath. About 14 hearts are needed for this project. Have the children glue the hearts onto the posterboard overlapping them until the entire frame is covered. The hearts are a symbol of the love we are to have for one another.

Then have five children cut out white paper doves as a sign of peace. The doves can be duplicated before class time and then cut out by the chilren. The doves are glued onto the wreath on top of the hearts.

The beautiful finished project is a peace wreath that is displayed in the classroom for all to see. It is a reminder that as Christians we are called to be a people of peace. We are to work toward peace in the world for all people.

Directory

Songs:

Hi God, Hi God 2, Hi God 3 by Carey Landry
A Dwelling Place by the St. Louis Jesuits
North American Liturgy Resources
10802 North 23rd Avenue
Phoenix, Arizona 85029
(800) 528-6043

*Jesus Is With Us, Jesus and His Friends, Living God's Word,
Celebrating God's Life* by Lou Fortunate
William H. Sadlier, Inc.
11 Park Place
New York, New York 10007
(800) 221-5175

Joy Together
Winston Press
P.O. Box 1630
Hagerstown, MD 21741
(800) 328-5125

Children's Books:

I Can Talk to God Anytime, Anyplace by Jennie Davis
Scripture Press Publications, Inc.
1825 College Avenue
Wheaton, Illinois 60187
(800) 323-2608

Plays:

Child's Play by Rev. David B. Gamm
Ave Maria Press
Notre Dame, Indiana 46556
(219) 287-2831

Notes

1. *St. Francis of Assisi: Omnibus of Sources*, Franciscan Herald Press, Chicago, IL. Used with permission.

2. Patricia Mathson, "Which Saint Am I?" *Religion Teacher's Journal* (October 1985), p. 7.

3. From *Craft Fun With Stickers*, by Shirley Beegle. © 1986. The Standard Publishing Company, Cincinnati, Ohio. Division of Standex International Corporation. Used by permission.

4. Edward Hays, *Prayers for the Domestic Church* (Easton, KS: Forest of Peace Books, Inc., 1979), p. 103.

5. Patricia Mathson, "Advent Family Day," *Today's Parish* (October 1983), p. 20.

6. Mary Jo Smith and Jerelyn Helmberger, *Who Am I?* (Chicago, IL: Loyola University Press, 1986), p. 125.

7. Elizabeth O. Thomas, "A Christmas Worship Service," *Church Teachers* (November–December 1979), p. 93.

8. Patricia Mathson, "Lessons from St. Blase," *Religion Teacher's Journal* (February 1985), p. 42.

9. Elaine M. Ward, *Be and Say a Fingerplay* (Brea, CA: Educational Ministries, Inc., 1982), p. 6.

10. Marcella Bush, "A Very Special Meal," *Religion Teacher's Journal* (March 1981), p. 10-11.

11. Ann Elliott, *Eyes to See God* © 1977 Morehouse–Barlow Co, Inc. Wilton, Connecticut, p. 82.

12. Pat Corrick Hinton, *Prayer After Nine Rainy Days and Other Family Prayers* (Minneapolis, MN: Winston Press, 1978), p. 50.

13. Patricia L. Mathson, "Prayer Ideas," *Catechist* (July/August 1985), p. 33.

14. Mary Jo Smith and Jerelyn Helmberger, *Who Am I?* (Chicago, IL: Loyola University Press, 1986), p. 128.

15. Carole MacKenthun, R.S.M. and Paulinus Dwyer, O.P., *Peace* (Carthage, IL: Shining Star Publications, 1986), p. 32.